D1232457

turn your back
on the problem

turn your back
on the problem

malcolm smith

THE BROTHERHOOD OF ST. ANDREW
BOOK SHOP
373 W. MARKET ST.
YORK, PA.   PH. 848-2137

LOGOS INTERNATIONAL
Plainfield, New Jersey 07060
Printed in the United States of America

© 1972 by
LOGOS INTERNATIONAL
PLAINFIELD, NEW JERSEY

ALL RIGHTS RESERVED
Printed in the United State of America
Library of Congress Catalog Card Number 72-87327
International Standard Book Number: 0-912106-34

Introduction

I was flying from California to New York recently, reading the manuscript of this book, when the stewardess glanced at me with concern. Tears were running down my face. She may have thought I was sad, but in reality I was rejoicing at the wonderful truths I was reading.

Malcolm Smith nearly gave up the ministry, and his discouragement is exactly what so many of us have felt, as we try to live a good life. At the end of the road are fatigue, defeat, self-pity, and a sense of inadequacy and failure.

At last, for Malcolm Smith, came the glorious understanding of *why* God had allowed him to work his way into a dead-end street. His rediscovery of God's wonderful purpose for His children and His church will be marvelous Good News for multitudes of weary Christians.

Turn Your Back on the Problem brings a practical, Twentieth-century revelation of *how* God intends to build His church — and His Kingdom on earth. As you read, you, too, will sense the joy and peace that comes when *God* does the doing and the building.

Should you happen to be on a dead-end street faced with your own inadequacies and towering problems, rejoice! You are in exactly the place where God can show you how exciting and glorious His ways are!

Merlin Carothers

A Note of Praise

I suppose I knew a year and a half ago that one day the Lord would have me write this book, but I had no idea when or how. I did know that I was not a writer and possessed no natural ability whatever, nor had I ever had the slightest yen to become one.

But I do have a super-natural Director, in the person of the Holy Spirit, and in God all things are possible. It took Him moving in a number of obedient servants, and I praise Him for first leading Art Duble of Logos Tapes to encourage me to actually put the story down on paper. He then led Dan Malachuk, the publisher of Logos International, to provide the incentive of a contract — on faith, really, since I had nothing to show. Then David Manuel, my editor, spent hours advising and encouraging; without his unstinting help the book would never have come to birth. I praise God for Marian Fauske, who was led to type the manuscript, and then cheerfully re-typed the whole thing after we had finished revising.

Most of all, I thank and praise Him for my wife Jean, who has been ... well, all that she has been during the years recorded in these pages.

Malcolm Smith
Brooklyn 1972

1

Weak sunlight filtered through the stained-glass windows, making a soft, colored pattern on the center aisle. Outside, a fire truck sped by, its siren screaming. Two others followed in rapid succession, shattering the peace of the church sanctuary.

Children played nearby, shouting in high-pitched Spanish. A subway train rumbled somewhere under the church. Brooklyn, 1970—a place that had wrapped itself around my heart in the last two years. But a place that had broken me and brought me to this desperate afternoon in late November.

Salem Gospel Tabernacle, on Fourth Avenue, in the Bay Ridge section of Brooklyn, had been a solid expression of the Evangelical Pentecostal witness for forty-five years. Started by a group of enthusiastic young folk, mostly Norwegians, it had its beginning in a hired

1

hall, but as new converts swelled their numbers, they soon moved their church to a permanent building. In 1942, they took the grand step of faith and bought a Jewish synagogue—that was to be their permanent home. There had been blessed years in the fifties, when the building was packed to the doors.

But in recent years, the area had followed the pattern of New York City, and became a low-rent housing area, filled with filth, junked cars, garbage and an ever-moving, seething mass of humanity.

What once had been a beautiful church on a tree-lined avenue, now stood forlorn on its corner—blown with old newspapers and broken beer cans. The streets, potted with holes and unfinished repairs, added to the desolate appearance of the scene. It was natural for young couples to move away in large numbers, until only a handful of the original number were left.

The balcony of the church, which had once been filled with people, was now unused—except on convention days. The main auditorium was seldom full. In fact, the whole interior seemed to share something of the bleakness of the neighborhood. But for the tenacious faith of the few that were left, the doors would have been closed long before.

In March of 1968, two and a half years earlier, my Trans-Atlantic plane felt its way down through the smog and landed at Kennedy International Airport. I had my first glimpse and smell of New York City. I was arriving to lead a one-week crusade at Salem, and David Kyvik, one of the younger elders of the church, met me at the airport. With him was E. C. Erikson, the interim pastor of Salem at that time—an old warrior of a minister, who had been praying night and day for a revival in Brooklyn.

As we drove along one of the main arteries into the city, I looked out the window at a sight that I would never get used to: Cars abandoned on the side of the parkway, stripped of wheels, battery, seats, etc.—and then demolished by bored teenagers. Enormous pieces of litter. The smog in the air made my eyes burn and water. I scanned the high-rise apartment buildings crowding the parkway. A few hours before, I had been in a quiet, leafy village of England. There were more people living in one of these apartment buildings, than in the whole village.

I looked at my driver, and said: "David, does anyone live here by choice?" He laughed, but I was grimly serious, and looking forward to the time when I would be headed in the opposite direction—back to England.

Before the end of that week, I knew I would be living in Brooklyn by choice. It came upon me with sure conviction that God was calling me to pastor this church. We sat in the study at the end of the final service of the crusade—the three elders of the Church, and myself. David Kyvik, who had met me, and who would become one of my closest friends; Alvig Hansen, one of the pioneers and charter member of the church, a man I would come to love and regard as a father; and Emil Bredstrand, a fine forthright man who took the floor and abruptly asked if I would be willing to consider a call to the pastorate of the church.

For a number of years,. my wife Jean and our three children had traveled with me from church to church, to camps, retreats, and conventions conducting special services. As we sat in the study that Friday night in 1968, I knew God had called us to cease our traveling and take this place to our heart. I told the Elders that I would be willing to consider a call, if they would extend it to me. And when I arrived back in England, the letter of call was already waiting for me.

So, on a steamy first of July of the same year, three excited children, one seasick wife, and a wondering me, stood in front of the desk of the Immigration Officer, on the deck of the S.S. *France.* He stamped our papers officously, and extending his hand said, "Welcome to the USA, Reverend!" The officer beside him added, with a smile in his voice, "And welcome to Brooklyn, a place that ain't quite like any other part of the USA."

We stepped onto the dockside, and after collecting twenty pieces of luggage, finally walked into the arms of a waiting church, who stood clustered around the barrier—waving, laughing and crying.

We had come, secure in God's call, and looking forward to the work to be done. The church needed a revival, and Brooklyn needed to know God. All of New York City spread before me. Its towering buildings, its migrant masses of people, its solid miles of traffic—people, people who needed to know God. And the Gospel I preached was the answer to every problem. It really was! It was only a matter of getting that Gospel to them—and we had plenty of ideas for accomplishing that. Years of traveling had made us experts in the field of communications.

As Alf Paulsen, who was to become a trusted friend and brother, drove us from the dockside, and through the

Battery Tunnel, I was like a rodeo horse, waiting to get out and run. I longed to show this city just what Jesus Christ could do.

Now it was November—a little over two years later. The emergency siren of the fire truck faded into the hum of the New York traffic. The subway was quiet, and the children had gone, and I was at the end of the road. I could not go on. I was a total failure. A failure in my ministry, in my personal life, in everything. The only honest thing I could do was resign the ministry and enter some secular field.

Slowly I got up from my knees, where I had been praying in front of the pulpit. How I loved this church. Light, spacious and warm, every pew seemed to reach out to me, as did the hearts of the people. I walked up the three steps to the platform. The whole church seemed alive. I am not a sentimental person, but as I stood there, I could feel already the service tomorrow morning. Doris Wahlberg would be playing the piano, as she had done for almost the life of the church. She would get the people really singing, as she always did. Ruth Larsen would be at the organ—quiet, faithful Ruth, just sitting there, radiating the fact that Jesus was alive. Bob Larsen, the choir leader, would come to the platform, give my shoulder a squeeze, and make our choir sing like angels—better than any professional choir I had heard. And Floyd Nicholson, my assistant, who had been with me for a few months, would step up and lead the congregation in hymns of praise.

I gave a long sigh, that was more a sob than a sigh,

and discovered that I loved these people even more than I realized, and not one of them would believe me when I stood tomorrow and told them I was going to resign.

I walked slowly over the empty platform in the failing light of early evening and down the back stairs. Every step had a memory from the packed months behind me. Two years before, I had ascended these stairs, full of ideas and promise. Now I went down them a broken man.

Walking across the basement floor, I fumbled for my keys, and smiled; I had gotten used to locking and unlocking every door. This great city, with all its drug addicts, thieves, and violence, had become part of my life.

I unlocked the door of my study. The walls of grained wood made it cozy—a place I loved to be in. The desk top was barely visible under all the papers and scribbled notes. Books lay open. Bibles and translations lay within groping distance on the green rug, where I seem to have wound up doing most of my research. The filing cabinet was open with some files half out. A mess perhaps, but a comfortable one. . .the notes that would make up tomorrow's sermon somewhere on the desk.

In the corner of my office, sticking out from behind the filing cabinet, was a large red heart—a gift from the teens last Valentine's Day, of Snoopy, with the inscription "Happiness is having a pastor called Malcolm Smith." I loved those kids—but I knew it would take more than love at this point.

I put a piece of paper into my typewriter and stared at it. How could I express the emptiness, the fear, the bitterness, that I felt at that moment? Slowly I began to type the letter that I would read the following morning to the elders, and later the same day to the whole church. Every word was wrung out of my heart, leaving some part of me punched into the paper:

Brethren:

When I came to this church, I did so with a very clear idea of what needed to be done. The church needed to be built up spiritually, its people filled with the Holy Spirit. They needed to be taught to be a praying people, to work together in harmony and unity, introducing the community to Jesus Christ. I do not deny that this has been accomplished in a few persons, but it is overwhelmingly true that in most cases, it has not. Nor does it look as though it will be.

By the end of June of this year, I was frustrated. A spiritual paralysis was creeping over me, and over the church. The congregation was listening and enjoying what was being said; some were helped, but very little was getting through. Now, we see a church that has in it dissension, complaint, unlove, discontent, prayer-lessness, no one being filled with the Holy Spirit, and hardly anyone being brought to know Jesus Christ. And my being the spiritual leader in this situation is worsening rather than helping it. More than any of you, I myself am in need of a spiritual revival—a revival I cannot find.

I feel this more deeply than I can put in words. It would be too easy to blame this or that. I know where the blame belongs, and therefore I give my resignation to this assembly, and will be leaving after the end of February of next year.

This decision has not been brought about by a call elsewhere.

We wish to thank you as a congregation with all our hearts, for the way you have loved us, and ministered to us. We shall never forget you.

Yours sincerely in Christ,

2

Laying the letter of resignation on my desk, I leaned back and put my hand over my eyes. Fifteen years lay behind that letter.

I was born in London in 1938 shortly after the beginning of World War II. My mother told me later of the urgency, fear, tension and harshness of those days. My father would be gone for weeks and months at a time, as a fire-fighter in Greater London, during those days of Hitler's outpouring of hatred.

A hardness—a kind of stoic acceptance coupled with determination was common to a Londoner during the Blitz. Walking through the rubble from the previous night's bombing, digging the dead out of the bomb craters, listening carefully for the moans and cries of those who may yet be alive, was the morning-by-morning occupation of the London cockney. Night after night, my mother pulled me from bed to rush to the steel shelter in the living room, where we waited while high above night bombers droned on unperturbed by searchlights or ground flak, dumping their tons of house-bursting explosives. One of my earliest memories was of seeing what seemed to be all of London a sea of fire, raging and storming, as we watched from our home in the suburban hills.

Before the end of the war, we moved to the mouth of the River Thames, to a seaside resort, Southend-on-Sea, in Essex. My parents had purchased a modest tourist home, and it took all their attention throughout the summer and fall.

The protective shell that the war had caused to grow around me was strengthened as I played with my cousins on the gray sands of the river. It was a Coney Island kind of resort, and we played the long summer days to the endless rinky-dink tunes of the amusement park, and the pervading smell of frying fish and chips.

When I was ten, new neighbors—church-going neighbors—moved next-door to us. They had a concern for the little pagan running wild next door, and made it their business to take me to Sunday School. It was a Sunday School of the Plymouth Brethren—and it was there that I first heard the Good News of Jesus Christ.

In this little mission school, Jesus Christ was not a pale anemic figure, gazing wanly through the mists of history. He was proclaimed as the Son of God—who had actually died on the cross my sins 2,000 years ago. What's more, He had risen from the dead, and was alive right now, in the twentieth century. Most important of all, whoever called upon Him would be saved. He could enter my life, free me from my guilt, and from the power of sin.

I did not hear of this at first, as I sat in that Sunday School class week after week,—but it began to come through.

Jesus emerged out of the dust of the past, and I knew in my young heart that He was there, alive. Someone would come into my heart, and direct me as to what life was all about—and at ten years of age, I was not too sure what it was all about.

Thus was kindled the spark of a desire. Vaguely I realized that He was the key of life, and I wanted Him. That spark propelled me forward into a prayer room one afternoon, after the Gospel had been told us yet again. The teacher was about to explain to us what it meant to give our lives away to Jesus—when a relative suddenly arrived and called me home.

I went for four more years doing many things—and being kept from doing many things—living in the twilight zone of knowing that Jesus Christ was real, without knowing Him personally.

My aunt was working in a print shop, and often came home with strange stories of the faith of those she worked with. They were Christians—but very different from the reserved, slightly stuffy kind that I had known in the Plymouth Brethren.

"They're praying for the sick," my aunt would report. "And you should hear the miracles that are happening! They were talking in the tea break about a man who was healed of blindness." And so she would go on, still in her work clothes, about the things she had heard at work that day. At these times, my mother looked skeptical, and rather nervous. "Well, it sounds like spiritism, if you ask me." She had a church background from her youth, before she married my father—who had no faith and didn't want any. She knew enough to beware of spiritism.

My aunt kept talking. "They keep inviting me to come to the services, and I hate to keep putting them off." She sipped her tea. "They say there is a missionary coming next week who had his insides taken out, and after prayer, he got them all back again—through a miracle. And," my aunt went on quickly, seeing my mother's expression, "he has X-rays to prove it!"

My mother shook her head, "You're kidding."

But she wasn't. The advertising came, and finally my mother decided to go to a service. Reluctantly, fearful and nervous—as was my habit of life, I went with her. My father stayed home. Only once had he gone to church—to the Plymouth Brethren—and had fallen asleep during the service. In the silence of the meeting, he had snored his way all the way to the closing hymn. He was left at home after that.

This church was very different. Long before we got to the door, we heard them singing—and they were clapping! A deacon greeted us at the door with the largest smile, and a firm handshake. We sat in amazement as they sang, stood and testified. All about us, everyone was hilariously happy.

Suddenly everyone was still, as a foreign language began to be spoken, by someone on the other side of the congregation. Like someone reading poetry, it rose and fell with feeling, the cadence steady, the syllables clear. I didn't understand it, but it was beautiful.

Turn Your Back on the Problem

My mother leaned over to me. "We're getting out of here! It's Catholic—they're chanting in Latin!" She hardly got the words out, when the pastor began to speak in a crisp, firm voice. We seemed to understand that he was interpreting the message of the foreign tongue. My mother froze and bowed her head, as the pastor described a life that had once known God—and gone far away from Him, and this night was confronting Him, who loved.

It was the story of mother's life—and she bowed and broke before God.

I sat nervous, uncomfortable, but impressed. That night my mother began to come back to the God she once knew. A few days later, the whole church joined in prayer for my father—and he came to know Christ in the living room of our home. Everything was changed and new and fresh for him. He testified that the sky was more blue, and the grass more green since Christ came in.

I went with them to the church. It was a Pentecostal church that we had stumbled on. They enjoyed their Christianity. They loved to sing, loud hallelujahs filled the air, and general joy was everywhere. These people were different from the Brethren. There was an indescribable difference—a power, a presence that filled their services. When there was a sick one, they prayed, and miracles did take place. And there were the strange tongues and interpretations.

They believed the same as the Brethren, but more. They believed that Jesus Christ introduced the Holy Spirit, and that this was a second experience after the first acceptance of Jesus as Lord. They called it the Baptism in the Holy Spirit, and it meant to know the Holy Spirit as He was known and experienced in the New

Testament. And the first miracle was the speaking in a new language. The miraculous tongue was essentially a prayer and worship language that made possible the fellowship and communion with God reflected in the pages of the New Testament letters. This new baptism experience provided the power for real service—the power to communicate Jesus Christ.

It was all very nice—but I wanted no part of it. The fears and inhibitions that had been etched into my very being as I had been hurried down dimly lit stairways to shelter from pounding bombs had become part of my life. I wanted no part of such an outgoing demonstrative religion. I could never see myself in the role of a tongue-speaking Pentecostal. If I was going to church at all, it would be with the Brethren—quiet, conservative. A place where a man could disappear into the furniture, and never be noticed.

It was one morning about this time, as my parents were coming to know Christ, that one of those almost ridiculously insignificant coincidences occurred—the sort that have a way of changing lives. I was wandering aimlessly along the crowded waterfront. It was a bright, hazy, dreamlike summer day. The fish-and-chips smell mingled with tar and oil slick from the boats on the river-side and the tangy seaweed. Milling crowds from London thronged the sidewalk—more than a few of them drunk, searching for something they seemed unable to define, let alone find. As if to help them, speakers were standing on boxes expounding on every subject under the sun—and most of them were drunk, too. I was amusedly watching one fellow with an audience of two, sawing away at the air as if he held all of Albert Hall spellbound, when someone thrust a booklet into my hand. It was a Gospel tract, I could see that. I shrugged and put it in my pocket.

When I arrived home an hour before lunch, the house was empty. Having nothing better to do, I pulled the booklet out of my pocket, and started to read.

I had heard it all in Sunday School long before—but now, suddenly, it became alive. God was speaking within me. I was a sinner. I had turned to my own way. I stood guilty, and for the first time in my life, I felt it deeply. Way down inside, I started trembling—and I couldn't stop. As I read on, the Good News became so real that I could almost see it happening. Jesus, the Son of God, had taken my place. He could—He was Man, and He was God. My sin had been laid upon Him. He had taken my punishment. The shedding of His Blood was the payment for my sin. He is alive! He arose from the dead—Lord and Savior from all sin. And no sooner did I know He was alive, than I somehow knew He was in the room where I was reading. I dropped to my knees, and called upon Him to come into my life and save me.

As I opened my eyes, the clock on the mantel struck noon—and the sun streamed in through the window onto the old chair by the radio. I had committed my life to Jesus. He was my Savior, and my Lord.

In the weeks that followed, my parents continued to enthusiastically attend the Pentecostal church. Sometimes I would go with them—still very afraid of what I saw and heard. But more and more I went to the Brethren Mission.

Then one day, at my parents' church, my mother was sitting next to me when, for no apparent reason, she began to weep ... and then she started to praise God quietly. I shifted uncomfortably. She began to cry and praise God louder.

Now I was deeply embarrassed and squirmed in my seat. But everyone else praised God and was thrilled. They knew what was happening: she was receiving the Baptism in the Holy Spirit. And I knew something else: this was the last time I would ever again come to this church.

The early hours of the next morning I heard my mother praying in the kitchen. I had heard her before, but this time she was praying in a new language. I lay and listened, quietly afraid of this supernatural that was happening all around me.

Some time later, a friend of mine at the Brethren Mission became sick with stomach ulcers. Colin was a special friend, and I was as concerned as he. He was scheduled for surgery in a few weeks when he asked me to go to the Pentecostal church in the next town of Westcliff, where he had heard that they prayed for the sick.

Reluctantly, I went with him.

The church was a small and unpretentious hall on a side street. Its long, narrow interior had a thin aisle down the center. On either side were chairs filled with people, singing and praising God, their faces beaming.

I slipped into a seat near the back, mentally planning my escape route if things became too personal, or too hot. I found myself afraid of the uninhibited joy of these people.

Then the preacher began to speak to the unconverted, and as he did so, I could not get away from it: God began to speak unmistakably to me. I couldn't close my ears or tune out; it was deep inside, and the words came clearly into my understanding.

You have searched for Me—longed for Me with all your heart.

I nodded and bowed my head. For weeks I had been praying and waiting on God, often late into the night. The Bible had become almost my only companion. I memorized large portions, meditating and asking God for a fulfillment of the promises. Because I knew that there had to be more than I had.

And there were cries to God, cries that I could not express, burdens of prayer that could not be released in the dimension of prayer. These longings had driven me to wait on God—for weeks now.

Yet, at the same time, you are fighting Me.

Again I nodded. However badly I wanted Him, I had erected every conceivable barrier against the possibility of speaking in tongues, and worshiping God aloud. I wanted to know Him. I wanted to be filled with God, and enjoy His promises—but strictly on my own terms. And to be honest, I had been aware that a battle was going on within me, but now I had to consciously acknowledge it, however reluctantly.

The Voice persisted.

There is only one path.

Even as I still fought it, my resistance was weakening. Now that the truth had been uncovered, I knew that the outcome was inevitable. Jesus Christ was Lord, and I knew my heart had finally only one desire—to give in to Him. Yes, there was only one path: unconditional surrender.

Submit to Me. Come to Me on My terms.

That meant being willing to be a tongue speaking Pentecostal, to be a fool in the eyes of the world, and even the church. To be willing to surrender everything, all of my inhibitions and fears—all of myself—to Him.

I sat back, understanding in a deeper way what it meant to be a disciple of Jesus Christ. He had died for me, my substitute, but to believe upon Him meant more than forgiveness; it meant that I became united with that death. It was to die to self-will, and my rights to my life, that He might live through me.

A text was painted on the wall in fading colors. "I am crucified with Christ; it is no longer I who live, but Christ who lives in me; and the life I now live in the flesh I live by faith in the Son of God, who loved me and gave himself for me. Gal. 2:20." I understood it on an experiential level a little more than I had ever done before. Crucified with Christ! I had no more rights to my life than a dead man would have. The Holy Spirit was now forcibly reminding me of this and bringing me to act in the light of it.

Bowing my head I said, "Yes Lord, I submit—I want You at any cost, and on Your terms."

Suddenly, I felt that Glory of God descend upon me . . . and at the same time, I heard the preacher say, "Shall we pray?" As he prayed over the congregation, he spoke to those who needed Christ as Lord and Savior—while I sat in the back of the church, totally

18

immersed in His love, and with the overwhelming love of Him welling up inside of me like a mighty river about to burst its dam and flood the valley. Almost as an afterthought, he summoned those seeking the Baptism in the Spirit, to join him in an adjacent room.

I was out of my seat like a shot. I ran into the room and hit the floor on my knees, praising God, and worshiping Jesus—and then out of my innermost being flowed a river of love heavenward, in a language I never had learned,—a beautiful, sufficient language that said all that my heart longed to say, although my mind did not understand the words. As the river flowed over me, through me, and out of me, I was cleansed and healed within. Inhibitions and fears, as old as the Blitz, torments and self-consciousness—all were swept away. The Holy Spirit had come, and He flowed through the corridors of memory, into every room, healing and making all things whole. After an hour or so, I gradually became quiet, and knelt worshiping the Lord in dumb silence. I was in a little wooden room—with a crude light hanging from the ceiling and an old green carpet on the floor. Hymnals that looked a hundred years old were piled around me. I grinned; to me, it had become the gate of heaven.

I turned to see who else was still in the room—and saw Colin, now healed and likewise baptized.

We slowly got to our feet and went out into the now empty and darkened main hall. We made our way up the aisle, slightly staggering under the Glory and Love that possessed us. A pastor from a church outside of town stood at the door. "So," he said, taking one look at us, "you met God tonight. Well, hallelujah!"

"Hallelujah, brother!"

Turn Your Back on the Problem

"Would you preach for me on Sunday night?" He stood silhouetted against the streetlight—key in hand, waiting. His question was addressed to me.

"Preach? I'll do anything you want me to, brother—just give me the address."

Time and place established, we got on our bikes and headed home, singing as we wove through the deserted streets, weaving patterns in the road with our cycles. We acted with sheer uninhibited joy—laughing and shouting praises to God. We were drunk—with the new wine of the Holy Spirit.

My mother met me at the door, her eyes shining. "I already know! I was praying, and the Lord told me."

I went to my room, and reaching for a blanket to wrap around me against the winter cold in the unheated room, I knelt down beside my bed. Suddenly, I gasped: I was committed to preach on Sunday!

In an instant, all sense of blessing vanished. But instead of the icy grip of fear I became aware of an absence of all natural emotions, a supernatural calm had settled over me. God had gotten me into this, and somehow He was going to see me through.

On an impulse, I reached for my Bible, and flipped it open to Acts 1:8—"After that the Holy Ghost is come upon you, ye shall receive power and be witnesses unto me." I put my hand on it, and said. "Thank You, Father. I don't feel anything, but You are Truth, and I receive what You say—even though I have no feelings. You have given me power to share You with the world."

I buried my head in the quilt on my bed, and praised God in faith.

Turn Your Back on the Problem

Sunday dawned cold and clear, not a cloud in the sky. Scrubbed and shining in our best suits, Colin and I headed out to Ashington, half an hour away by bike. In those days, it was an untouched country village and a few scattered farms. As we pedaled down the lane that ran through frosted fields and over frozen streams, our breath came out in puffs, like smoke from the stack of a far-away steam engine. I knew we weren't supposed to be nervous, but after four days of frantic rehearsing, I couldn't help it.

The church came into sight, a small, wood-frame structure in a large field. We leaned our bikes against an old oak tree and hurried up the mud-and-cinder path. Inside, a few home-made benches were arranged in front of a crude pulpit which was covered with a blue velvet cloth and crowned by a massive black Bible.

I looked around—and my heart sank. The word had apparently gotten around that a kid of fifteen was going to be preaching. The place was full of teenagers, who would normally be hanging around outside the tavern.

His voice tremulous amid some cat-calls and jeers, Colin conducted the songs—that no one knew. This was it: I rose to speak the message that I had taken four days and nights to prepare, taking firm hold of the huge Bible to keep my hands from shaking.

The message exploded the moment I opened my mouth. Four minutes later, I had nothing left to say. I couldn't even pray. As the silence grew longer, my heart desperately reached out to the Holy Spirit. Abruptly, peace replaced panic, and the Glory, Love and Power began to build. The message assembled itself in my mind—and I preached for the next thirty minutes.

21

Turn Your Back on the Problem

At the end of the sermon, empowered to unbelievable boldness by the Holy Spirit, I dared to call to the altar all who would receive Christ—and five teenagers came forward. That night as Colin and I cycled home, hallelujahs again filled the still March air. He (God) had turned an introverted, fear-filled kid into a preacher.

I leaned back in my chair and stared up at the dark ceiling beyond the fluorescent lights in my office. That was sixteen years ago—my first sermon. My eyes came back to the letter of resignation on my desk. Tomorrow morning, I would preach my last.

I folded the letter, tucked it in my pocket, and went out onto the streets of Brooklyn. It was beginning to drizzle, and the trash-strewn streets were misty. A police car, lights flashing and siren screaming, careened around the corner and through the red lights outside the church, an ambulance right behind it.

3

It was already late when I let myself in. Moving like someone in a trance, and oblivious to whether anyone else might still be up, I wandered into the kitchen and leaned my forehead against the cold refrigerator door. I had taken my wife and children, and led them up a dead-end street. I had no idea where we were going from here. Jean's dedication to God, and her loyalty to me, deserved better leadership than that.

Jean and I had met in Bible School in England in 1956. I had gone there in 1955—the summer after I had received the Baptism in the Holy Spirit. The school, The International Bible Training Institute, was an old, slightly thread-bare, but still productive "gentleman's farm"—with a large drafty mansion and ten acres of woodland and pasture. The nearest sizable town was Brighton, a good ten miles away. We were steeped in the centuries-old atmosphere of the Sussex Hills—dotted with sleepy, bypast villages, complete with cobblestone streets and thatch-roofed cottages.

It was unlike many schools today. We had two full years of intense preparation for ministry, with days filled with studies, prayer, and worship. Our only recreation was to work in the vegetable gardens, milk cows, and feed the chickens and ducks. This school tried to be self-supporting; what didn't come from the land, we learned to pray in. It was a rigorous firsthand experience of living by faith, with the Invisible God to provide.

During my last year at school, a vivacious blue-eyed blonde, by the name of Jean Waters, arrived from Hastings, a sea-side town on the English Channel. As I came to know her, I was struck by the similarity of our backgrounds. Born just before the war, she, too, had grown into childhood feeling the earth shake. Directly opposite France, the little town of Hastings was one of Hitler's favorite targets. Most of the town's women and children were evacuated, to live in limestone caves that a century before had been used by smugglers. Sleeping on cots in the winding passages of the cave—she had learned young in life, the horrors of war. Later, Jean was separated from sisters and parents, and taken to Wales, to live with strangers—at a very young age, she had learned a great deal about loneliness. And so, she, too, had matured far beyond her sixteen years.

In 1956, living as a rebellious teenager in a pre-nursing school, she was taken by friends to hear Billy Graham, who was conducting his historic crusade in London's Harringay Arena. Going all that way to hear some American preacher was the last thing Jean wanted to do, but her friends had practically forced her into it.

But to her surprise the singing of Bev Shea gripped her, and Billy's sermon that evening was directed by the Holy Spirit straight to her softened heart. As the blond, square-jawed preacher asked for a decision, she was the first one down the aisle to receive Christ—her tears streaking her make-up as she ran. Later, she received the Baptism in the Holy Spirit, without knowing what had happened, let alone what it was called, until a friend pointed out the same experience in the Book of Acts.

She entered Bible School in 1956, without any clear idea of where she was going—except that God had His hand on her life, had, in fact, chosen her for some kind of special service. She washed her way through school—scrubbing and ironing the student's laundry, without the aid of modern conveniences.

We fell in love that year, and when I left school, I promised to return with an engagement ring.

Out in the ministry, though, away from the woods and lanes of Sussex, life came on like a wet washcloth in the face. My first assignment was a mission up in Norfolk, England—ten people who had tenaciously kept the doors of the tiny church open, without any hope of increase, were my congregation. Skeptical of what a seventeen-year-old kid could give them in the way of spiritual succor, they nonetheless agreed to pay me twelve dollars a week—for one week anyway. With that, I purchased a sleeping bag, and made my bed on the church platform. Sometimes I received the twelve dollars—but not always. They were fine people, but poor, and they did their best.

Many cold nights were spent on the bare boards of that platform, with only the increasingly thin padding of the sleeping bag between me and the hard floor. Many lonely meals consisted of a loaf of bread, and a bottle of milk. It seemed an impossible life. Again and again I was assailed with doubts—should I quit now and enter secular life? No, God had called me: there was no turning back.

One thought haunted me above all others: this was no place for a woman, especially that vivacious blonde, whom I had asked to marry me. Finally, I committed my thoughts to paper—carefully pointing out that the full-time service of Jesus demanded all we had. There was no money, no accommodations, few friends, many enemies, much persecution. Our only consolation was that He was with us always. In the light of this, I advised her strongly to leave me now, while the leaving was relatively easy, as I was determined to go on—at any cost.

Upon receiving the letter, Jean was certain that I was trying to give her up. With many tears she re-read the letter—and the girls in the dorm agreed that I was just trying to be rid of her. But in her heart the Holy Spirit showed her the truth of it. This was not a severing letter, but the stark reality of what serving Jesus Christ might well mean.

Quietly, she went to the school chapel, to let the Holy Spirit do some talking. Was she really willing to live a life like that? Alternating between anger at God that someone should be asked to live that way, and reluctant submission that said she would do anything He said, she went over and over it, each time learning a bit more about herself—and about Him. Finally, the Holy Spirit brought her to the place of real surrender. The place where she would gladly go anywhere, and do anything, content in the simple knowledge that it was His will.

Turn Your Back on the Problem

Filled with peace, she wrote back a note, saying that she was ready for even the sleeping bag. The God who was with one, could be with two.

The little mission to which I had been assigned was prospering. The Lord seemed able to use me, despite my age and inexperience.

After the mission was regularly filled, to the point where we had to have two services on Sunday nights to accommodate everyone who wanted to attend—I felt the Lord telling me my job here was done. When I left, the congregation gave me the unheard of gift of twenty pounds—about fifty dollars. I took a train to London, and then walked the forty miles to the Bible school, wondering the whole way what her reaction would be when I took her out to buy an engagement ring.

We set a date for our wedding, and made a list of all the things we needed. We prayed for each item, and the Lord provided to the last item—each one a miracle. Came the long-awaited day, and belatedly I realized that the one thing that we hadn't listed was the fare to take us on a honeymoon. I prayed desperately, but none of the cards or letters of well-wishers contained any money. We said good-byes to our friends, and left for the train station—without tickets, and with only a handful of change. It was hard not to panic, or at least succumb to feeling foolish, but we somehow knew that God would deliver us. Then, to our horror, the whole wedding party decided, on the spur of the moment, to come with us to the station.

Fifteen minutes before the train was due, I knew God was testing. I stepped in line to buy the tickets—with what? God would supply. Slowly the line moved toward the ticket window, until there were only two men ahead of me. Suddenly a car drove right into the station yard. My wife's pastor ran over to me, and pressed an envelope into my hand, saying, "A little gift from the church." Opening it, I praised God out loud, mindless of those standing within earshot. It contained just enough for our tickets.

During the days away I preached enough to buy the tickets home. Home was a two-room apartment in Stowmarket, a sleepy little market town in the heart of East Anglia. Farms dotted the country side, villages clustered by the side of narrow lanes that wound through pastures and wheat fields. It was a town with little or no preaching of the Gospel, and we were there to establish a church.

The two-room apartment where we were to live had been unused for years. Cobwebs lined the windows like silk curtains. The ceiling had fallen in, and in one musty room the paper hung off the walls. As we picked our way through the debris, we discovered a plaque hanging on the wall which said, simply, Hope thou in God. We rolled up our sleeves and did just that—and with the help of some of the new converts transformed the shambles into our first home. That was the beginning of our ministry together, and throughout Jean had been a seasoned soldier of Jesus Christ, never flinching.

In all our years together, Jean never claimed a special ministry—just to be my wife. I had assumed spiritual leadership, and she had followed. We had never had financial security, and many times we walked into impossible situations—but always, the lesson of the train station would repeat itself—God would meet us, and see us each step of the way.

Three children were born over the years. Donna, our eldest, was born in England. Karen came in Ireland, and finally Yvette was born in Seattle, Washington—while we were on a crusade. Together we traveled the highways of the British Isles, Canada, and the States. Suitcases, motels, warm Christian homes—all had been our shelter. Jean had bravely raised the children without the security or protection of a home of our own. Donna was once asked where we lived while we were traveling. Thinking for some time, she said, "We have a home, but we don't have a house to put it in."

Turning away from the refrigerator, and heading for our bedroom, I thanked God for my wife, who had stuck by me through everything. It would come as no surprise when I showed her the letter of resignation. She had been expecting it as she watched the pressure build up in me the last few weeks.

I noticed there was no light under the door, so I opened it softly, in case she was already asleep. But she turned on the light. "Can't get to sleep; is everything all right?"

"I'm resigning tomorrow morning." Her big blue eyes looked at me incredulously. "Darling, you really are?"—She took the letter, and read it slowly. We were deeply attached to Salem, more than to any other church or place we had ever been, but as I had anticipated she simply smiled and said, "Well, where are we going?"

The hurt—I didn't know. I told her so. She gave me a squeeze which let me know she was ready to come with me to the end of the world.

Turn Your Back on the Problem

Sleep did not come readily that night. In the next room, Donna was tossing in her sleep, making every spring creak. Yvette, the youngest, was having a dream and speaking garbled words. Beside me, Jean was breathing softly. And now I felt the fingers of fear closing around me. What was I doing? In nine hours we would be a little family precariously set adrift with no known destination. I fell into a fitful sleep.

"Mommy, where are my shoes?" Donna's words brought me to muzzy consciousness.

"Where you put them."

"I saw them in the basement," Karen said, trying to be helpful.

"What are they doing down there?"

"Mommy, there's no toothpaste."

"Mommy, which dress should I put on?"

"Why don't you wear your red one?"

"But I wore that one last week."

"Now all of you: Eat your breakfast—and clean your teeth, before Daddy gets in the bathroom."

The sounds of Sunday morning . . . how I loved them, and the family that made them.

Suddenly I was stricken with the thought of what the morning held. I had to resign. I lurched out of bed and entered into the pandemonium of children, clothes, corn-flakes and toothpaste. Finally the last tooth was brushed, the bathroom door was closed, and I could shave in peace. At least on the outside; within my mind I played over and over my imaginings of the details of the next few hours like a needle on a worn-out record.

Over a hurried breakfast of grapefruit and cereal, Jean and I finally talked about it.

Turn Your Back on the Problem

"I'm going to miss these people terribly." Jean looked at me wistfully. "They may have faults, but we are a part of them now; they are our people." I nodded, unable to add anything. Jean continued, "I committed it all to the Lord last night, I know the Lord will tell you what to do. I'm not worrying anymore—this is God's business."

I sensed that in the corner of her mind she was nonetheless dreading the possibility of traveling again, or another church to get adjusted to. And I knew, in a corner of my own mind, as I drank my tea, that it was going to be neither traveling nor a church—I was going to resign from the ministry entirely.

I picked up the telephone, and called Floyd, my assistant. We had talked before about the possibility of my resigning, and he had stubbornly refused to even consider it.

"Floyd, I am resigning this morning. I think you should be the first to know."

"What!" His usual unemotional voice registered shock. "You'll not carry it through, I know you will change your mind."

"I'm sorry. I don't think so." And my own voice started to go. "Look," I said crisply, "ask the Elders to meet me before Sunday School. I think it will be easier if you don't say anything to anyone beforehand."

All too soon, all were assembled in my office. Emil Bredstrand had since gone back to Sweden to live, which left David Kyvik, Alvig Hansen, and Paul Mathiesen, a new member on the board, sitting opposite me.

On the desk in front of me, was the letter.

I looked at the three men. I loved them. I didn't

know how I was going to read what I had to say. With a tight throat, I read what had been wrung out of my heart the night before. They wept, and so did I. We sat looking at each other through our tears. How could I tell them my whole heart—when I hardly knew it myself? They begged me to reconsider, to think for another week—but I knew there was nothing else to do.

Somehow, I preached through the service, and then invited the church members to meet with me in the basement. My eyes fell on each face as they filed into the basement fellowship room and quietly took their seats. They had no idea what was coming, but something in my announcement must have indicated a crisis for the usual light banter was lacking. How these people had entwined themselves around our hearts! They sat and talked in low tones while the congregation gathered. Jean disappeared into the kitchen at the rear of the basement, with Judy, Floyd's wife. Neither of them could bear to observe what was coming.

A quiet seemed to come of its own accord, and I arose and took the letter in my hand. It seemed that at that moment the people realized instinctively what was coming. I began to read, forcing the words out through my lips, each word another step out of the congregation. At the last word, I gave a sigh and looked over the congregation, strangely detached. I was on the outside, looking in.

The congregation broke, as one. Sobbing, some stood and asked me to stay. Others just wept where they sat. I stood frozen—unable to answer or even move. Fifteen years of ministry was dying—and I couldn't say or do a thing.

Turn Your Back on the Problem

Finally, the elders came up and took over the meeting. meeting. They urged me to go on a vacation—to think matters over. I just shook my head. There was nothing to think over.

But they gently pressed me to take the vacation that had long been due me, that I had never had a chance to take. Weeks of building fatigue seemed to pour in on me, and I became aware of how very tired I was. I wanted to get away and be alone. Without fully realizing what I was doing I told them that we would accept the vacation, on the condition that they understood that we were not reconsidering our decision.

4

The next few days passed almost as in a slow-motion dream. I was deadened, incapable of thinking, or even reacting. The one thing my mind fixed on was getting away. Quietly, Jean looked after all the details in the next few days, packing and preparing, arranging for Floyd and Judy to move into our house to look after the girls while we were gone.

I stopped to say good-by to Alf Paulsen, Chairman of the Trustee Board and David Kyvik at their paint store on Fifth Avenue.

"You'll be back," Alf said, nodding and smiling. "God has told me so." I just looked at him without speaking. Later, in the car, Floyd said the same thing.

"You'll see; after you've been down there a few days, I know you will come back." Again I said nothing, for by this time I was tired of pretending that there might be even a remote possiblity.

Turn Your Back on the Problem

We piled the luggage into the trunk of the car—kissed our three girls, and pulled onto the Belt Parkway to Kennedy Airport, half an hour from our home. It was a slick, gray day in November—with a light drizzle falling.

The huge Pan American building was a bustling, buzzing mass of people—all excitedly going somewhere. Pan Am posters shouted their "Escape Plan" from every billboard. Was this what I was doing? Was I a spiritual fugitive, escaping to the Virgin Islands, trying to escape from the inescapable? Angrily, I put it all out of my mind. I was going to leave all that behind, and really relax.

An intimate, yet strangely impersonal female voice announced the imminent departure of our flight. "Passengers for St. Thomas and St. Croix will please board through Gate Three."

We edged into the stream of affluent New Yorkers escaping to the sun. On board, we fastened our seat belts, and in minutes the big jet banked over the skyscrapers of Manhattan and headed south.

Those steel and glass fingers reaching up below me—five million people of all sizes and shapes, languages and colors—all jammed together on that little island. I realized how I had come to love it. As we soared higher, I actually began to relax. We plunged into a cloud layer, and outside the window everything was suddenly thick and creamy gray-white—then they were all below us like a billowy quilt, and there was nothing but clear blue sky and blazing sun.

We leaned back and looked at each other, and I couldn't help smiling. I pulled a letter out of my pocket. It was from Mary Ann Galati. Simple and powerful, it attested to the blessing we had been in her life, in sharing a verse from Philippians 4—when she had been going through a personal crisis: "... and the peace of God that passeth all understanding, keep your hearts and minds through Jesus Christ." She simply prayed that for us—and asked us to stay on. I passed the letter over to Jean, and let the problem disappear beneath the clouds.

We stepped out of the plane into almost indecently warm air, and bright—Jean reached into her purse and extracted *both* our sunglasses. A taxi took us across the island from the airport. On the way, the driver stopped to talk to friends, and again to buy some groceries. And I knew we had come to the right place to really unwind.

That afternoon, a tropical rainstorm lashed the island. There was nothing to do but lie on the bed, and maybe read, until it was over. The rain swept in from the sea in great waves, tearing at the windows, blotting out the hills around the bay—leaving us in a pocket of isolation.

I had come here to relax—to leave any thoughts a thousand miles behind—but the problem had apparently slipped unnoticed into our baggage, for here it was, big as life. The worn-out record started up again, and the same old thoughts churned around and around in my head. I groaned. Would I never be released from their shackles? Jean stirred in her nap, and I lay on my back, wide awake and envying her ability to sleep.

The white ceiling was as blank as my future, and almost seemed to be mocking me. The rain beat angrily at the veranda doors, as the surging frustrations beat against my mind.

Turn Your Back on the Problem

Did I really have a call to the ministry? How much was my motivation of God and how much youthful romantic idealism? Then a new thought came, worse than any of the others. Had God brought me to this place to show me that I had been believing a lie all these years? Like a hammer the thoughts beat angrily, yet pleading for answers.

I recognized fear rising deep within battling its way to the surface, and I felt suddenly small, groping for an answer, and half-afraid of finding it. Was I doubting my salvation? No! I knew my sins were gone—through the shed Blood of Jesus, and I was just as certain that I had received the Baptism in the Holy Spirit. But for the prayer language He had given me, I would never have lived through the last months.

It was the ministry that was at the heart of this fear. I had tried so much—and had failed so completely. We did not lack success, as the world counts success. We seemed to be in great demand to preach and lecture in churches, retreats and conventions; in fact, our schedule was so filled that we had to turn down invitations several months in advance. Proven programs and ideas for communicating Christ crammed my filing cabinet. And as for our congregation, well, their reaction to my announced departure spoke for itself.

But there was more to the ministry—to church—than success, techniques, and a good rapport with one's congregation. The early church, as described in the New Testament, was *alive*! God, by His Holy Spirit, was clearly at the helm. The men were completely yielded to Him and were thus used mightily by Him, and they were living demonstrations of their preaching.

Turn Your Back on the Problem

The preaching of the early disciples was incidental to their living. Whatever they said was first demonstrated in their lives. They preached that Jesus Christ had taken their sin and carried it away at the cross; that their old life died with Him there, and now alive in Him, they were under the direction of the Holy Spirit. But before they preached it, they demonstrated it in their lives. They were dead to sin, Christ shone through them; they lived their life at the dictate of the Holy Spirit. What they said and what they did were spontaneous expressions of who they were in Christ.

Did Christ shine through me? In my living was it the dictates of the Holy Spirit that ordered my life? How much of Christ had been been in me in the last year? I groaned. Each month there had been less and less of Him. I was becoming thoroughly professional. Suddenly the full horror of that thought hit me—a professional Pentecostal. Believing in the Holy Spirit, yet not having the evidence in my life or in my ministry. My life was now falling short of my own preaching; yet once, the preaching had been an almost incidental by-product of my life. But that seemed a thousand years ago.

I pulled myself up on the bed and reached for my Bible. Idly, I turned the pages of the Acts of the Apostles. What was locked up in the pages of that book that I could have missed? I had lived with the Bible for years, visited with the men who walked the pages of the New Testament, and had come to know them better than most people know their next-door neighbors.

I lay back and closed my eyes, and again saw Peter walking with John to the Temple to pray, confronting the man lame from birth. Again, there was the piteous cry for alms, and the bold words of Peter, "Silver and gold have I none, but such as I have, give I unto thee."

There it was! Authority—a boldness, an absolute assurance of what God was doing. A walking in harmony with God. An authority that I coveted and had prayed for, struggled to find, and from which goal I had fallen so hopelessly short. Standing before the millions of New York City, feeling so helpless and powerless. I looked into the eyes of these two fishermen from Galilee. The older Peter, the young John—if only I knew the where and the how of that boldness and authority.

I felt angry and afraid. Angry that I had searched the Bible for so long, and it had not been shown to me. Afraid that I would never find it . . . anywhere.

Incredibly I looked at Stephen as he died with the stones flying around him, and I envied him. I heard him pray that the sins of his persecutors would not be laid to their charge. I stood in the circle of grim-faced persecutors as they stooped and reached for rocks and straightened to take aim and threw, and quickly stooped again. I saw his face shining, almost with a radiance of its own, like an angel.

I looked with disgust at my life. I had preached consecrated, Christlike living, but my life was woefully short of it. Totally lacking in the degree of love young Stephen had. Very far short of shining like an angel.

"Dear Lord, I know all the words, and I know that they are truth—after all these years, I am still struggling so much, and failing so badly."

And now fear at the failure rose tightly within me, swelling in my chest cavity, till I could scarcely breathe.

Then there was the bold and determined preaching of

Philip as he went to Samaria. The results that come so easily, like ripened fruit from the vine. The obviously clear directions that he had. He knew that he was to be in Samaria. He knew when to leave. He knew where to go thereafter. He—they all flowed in the strength and wisdom of another.

Why hadn't I found that? Why had I struggled so hard to make that happen, and it never did?

I looked into the spray-spattered face of Paul on the deck of the rolling, pitching ship. Dark waves were breaking over the gunwales, the shrieking wind was tearing at the sails and rigging, and even the seasoned sailors were in the grip of panic and ready to abandon ship . . . but Paul *knew* the mind of God and spoke with such calm assurance that the rest seemed to know he knew.

I rolled over and buried my head in the pillow. Our own ministry had been so hit-and-miss, so seldom actually knowing the mind of God, as these men knew. It always seemed that when we worked in one place, God would be working somewhere else. Time after time we would see and read of all the wonderful things that God was doing—the miracles, the healings, the revivals—and redouble our efforts. I had run after every need in sight, and tried so hard to apply the truth to it . . . and I had failed. And it hurt and ached because I wanted so badly to do God's work.

Deep inside I sensed that if ever I was going to face the truth, it would have to be now, right here, with my wife drowsing beside me and the rain coming down in buckets. This was it.

The shell was there. The words and the actions. Day

41

after day, service after service, I went through all the motions, knew all the procedures.

I could so easily become a professional minister—I had in fact become one ... yet the real thing seemed a million miles away. That first sermon I had preached as a frightened, trusting, fifteen-year-old boy, was more anointed than any I had preached in a long time.

I reminded myself that this should be no surprise. I suppose I had seen it coming for years. But as we had traveled from crusade to crusade, it had been so easy not to see it. We could always find a good reason for the Living God not to be operating among us.

In one place it was the people; they didn't believe God, or they were not ready to hear what we said. In another church, there was not expectancy, no anticipation of the movement of the Spirit. The pastor and the people were dead. And conversely, there were still other places that had heard so much truth that they were no longer hearing. Always, there was a perfectly rational explanation for why there was none of the power that surged through the New Testament.

At the end of every crusade, every series of meetings, we would say that next time, at the next retreat, the next convention—*there,* we would see, and respond to, the Miracle-Worker of the Bible.

I knew that He was there, I had been used by Him just enough to really *know.* If I didn't, I would have resigned long before now. There would be the unexplainable explosion of God among us. It was then that I knew I was not chasing a phantom. And at such times, God was doing it, not me. There would be a supernatural ease in preaching and sharing Jesus. And people would suddenly see what I could never adequately explain. Expectancy rose in us and them spontaneously, without any exhortation—the intense concentration, the sharpened discernment, the hushed waiting for whatever God might do or reveal next. Faith was natural. And I would preach the same as ever—but something was different. The Holy Spirit was present, and He fired and quickened the Words. I knew what it could be . . .

Why aren't You there all the time? Why can't I always know You directing and helping me? Why were You always with the Apostles and New Testament Christians, and not with me? I pounded the bed with my fist, and Jean turned in her sleep.

My mind churned back through the years to those days when we did enjoy His abiding presence. We traveled the crusade circuit for a number of years with Caroll Forseth and his wife Vivian. They played Hawaian guitar and sang, Caroll painting lightning sketches that we gave away to the person bringing the most visitors to the service. We made a relaxed, well-balanced team and covered thousands of miles together. Caroll and I had driven for thousands of miles cruising along, talking these same questions over. Somehow we never seemed to reach any real conclusions, and then, when we despaired of finding any solution that we could hang onto, we would stumble on what we longed for.

There was that camp meeting outside of Spokane, Washington, in the summer of '65. Spelling each other at the wheel, we had driven nonstop for a thousand miles to be at the service on time. When we arrived, we were both exhausted, more asleep than awake. Getting out of our car, and walking to the platform, I begged the Lord to take over, as I was too tired to think. I looked over the crowded auditorium, filled with bored and restless teenagers. Some were chewing bubble gum and popping it, to the snickers of those around them. The last thing they were in a mood for was a sermon.

As I stood up and cleared my throat, I knew unmistakably that the Holy Spirit was there, that it was out of my hands. All I had to do was speak the words He gave me. I did. And suddenly, to my amazement, I watched a change come over that audience. Every last one was gripped, and some began to weep.

No sooner had I finished, than the prayer chapel was filled with teens, calling upon Christ for salvation, while others received the Baptism in the Holy Spirit. And this went on night after night, for the whole camp week. We just stood back in awe and watched God at work.

Later, after the last meeting was over, I sat on my bunk and cried to God, "What have I done here, that I haven't done in other places? Why such a sense of power here? What's the key that I'm not able to use elsewhere?"

But the answer had not come then—any more than it was coming now. The blank white ceiling stared down at me, and I rolled on my side to stare out the rain-streaked window, at the blank gray sky.

My mind went back to Liverpool, England. We had gone there on a crusade in 1966, to the Anglican parish church of St. Saviors in Everton. The regular congregation was all of about forty people. To be sure, the priest worked hard in preparation for our arrival, but no natural explanation could account for what happened. The first night, two thousand people jammed the building, and every night for a solid month, the building was packed. Hundreds committed their lives to Christ, and were filled with joy.

Many times during that month, I would slip into the old church by day, and walk its aisles. In that intense stillness, with the sun coming through the stained glass windows, playing soft rose and blue hues on the carved oak pews and worn carpeting, I would sit where perhaps half a dozen generations had sat, worshiping God. The lofty stone arches above seemed to echo my thankfulness to God for what He was doing, for the sovereign work of the Spirit in which I was allowed to participate. And I *was* thankful. Never had I been so used, and this is surely why we are on earth—to be fully used of God in glorifying Him. At those times, there were no words sufficient to express my praise to Him. And yet, even then, I could not refrain from asking why it didn't happen every time. And again, the stillness gave no answer.

Some had tried to counsel me. To be used of God in leading others to experience Him was not always our lot. Sometimes we would have to preach the truth and leave others to harvest the results. That was obvious, but to sow the seed of truth in hearts, without seeing immediate results, would be as exciting as reaping those results if it was accompanied with a sense of His Presence and direction.

And my thoughts went round and round, tracking in the familiar groove: You know Jesus is alive. You know His Blood cleanses from all sin. You have been baptized in the Holy Spirit. You have spoken in tongues. You pray. What is it, then, that Paul and Stephen and Peter

45

and James and all the others knew, that you don't know?

Coming to Brooklyn had been the final challenge. Its filthy, run-down streets reflected empty, confused, futile lives. And so did the lonely faces, frightened eyes, and clenched fists gripping the straps of the screaming subway. Meaningless, fearful existence, shoved and pushed on crowded streets through crowded lives. If the Gospel was for real, here was the place to prove it.

We had thrown everything we had into it. Every spiritual muscle was strained to the limit. And it turned out like our crusades—successful on the outside, hollow on the inside—only this time I couldn't run to the next one.

Attendance had increased, the congregation was helped, and most of the people seemed quite content. But on my corner of Brooklyn, I knew that the New Testament kind of church was not being built, however hard I had tried. In Brooklyn, I took a hard look at my own life—and could scarcely bear to face what I saw.

The fault could not be laid to others, nor to circumstances: I alone was to blame. Always in the past I had been able to shift much, if not all, of the blame to others, and vaguely hope that something would happen down the road. Well, this was the end of the road. Nothing had happened, nothing was about to happen, and the only honest thing I could do was resign.

The rain was finally abating. I glanced at my watch: two hours had passed, and I was right back at the beginning. Only now I was just that much more tired of it all, that much more convinced that there was no solution for me but to quit the charade and get out of the ministry. At least I would not be a hypocrite, and whited sepulchre. And in my mind I was no longer a minister.

5

The next few days were a sleepwalk of eating, lying on the beach, walking aimlessly through endless back streets and bazaars of the little town, and falling into a fitful sleep at night.

The harder I tried not to think, the more the same old thoughts came to haunt me, so that instead of relaxing, I grew increasingly angry and uptight. The cab drivers were stupidly slow, the tourists, in my eyes, invariably exhibited the worst traits of tourists, restaurant service seemed almost deliberately bad, and I found myself snapping irritably at everybody and everything. Gradually I retired into silence, spending more and more time in our room, lying on the bed brooding. I knew that I was slipping into a black abyss, and as in a nightmare, I seemed powerless to do anything to prevent it.

On top of everything else, I was aware that I was ruining the first real vacation that Jean had ever had, and the thought only made me resent her for making me feel guilty. Our once-in-a-lifetime vacation—and I was as bored as if we were walking around Woolworths.

If only I could muster a little happiness for her sake. After all her loyalty and love and patience, she really deserved something better. At the very least I should try to let her in on the madness that was going on inside of me, and when I looked at her, her eyes told me how much she yearned to help. But this was my hell and I was not about to drag her into it, though it hurt more to know the rejection she must be feeling.

One evening at dusk we sat at dinner on the veranda overlooking the bay. Palms and vines swept down the cliffs to almost engulf us, and rush on their way to the sea far below. The air was fragrant with the aroma of exotic flowers, and in the distance were the faint cries of strange birds. I picked at my steak without raising my eyes and made an effort to break the silence. "What do you think we should do?"

"The Lord will tell you what you should do," Jean said quietly. "Don't worry, everything will be all right—and you know that whatever you have to do, I'm happy to follow you."

I nodded, inwardly wishing that He would let me know.

With a week still to go, we met another couple who enjoyed all the things that I was bored with. I could see the Lord's hand in that, and I had the grace to thank Him; at least Jean's memories of this trip wouldn't be entirely wretched.

We went to the beach as a foursome. The day was so bright, it seemed polished—just the sort that the travel posters implied occurred daily. It was hard to remember that it was December. We walked slowly, feeling the sand hot between our toes. A hot-dog stand wafted a smell reminiscent of Coney Island among the palm trees, and on the roof of the stand, a radio loudspeaker filled the air with "I'm Dreaming of a White Christmas." For no reason, the whole affair made me angry, as practically everything did these days. This time I felt anger inside me that anyone would desecrate this beach with that greasy smell and ridiculous noise. I felt like hurling the hot-dog grill to the ground and getting a stick to smash the speaker, and I was afraid, because I knew how close I was to doing just that.

I picked my way over and through the sunbathing crowds, and my boyhood days on the beach at Southend came rushing back. I was a little child again, playing in the sand, with all the crowds around and the smell of fish and chips.

We finally left it all behind—the crowds, the smells, and the music. Nothing but deserted beach stretched before us. The gently undulating sand shimmered white in the blazing sun, as the cobalt blue waves of the lagoon splashed on the beach below us. There was no breeze; the palms, in whose shade we walked, were so still, the whole scene could have been a snapshot.

Jean and the others went in for a swim. I excused myself, wandered a ways down the beach, and lay down under the palms, folding a towel for a pillow. Far above, the interlaced palm fronds made a checkered pattern against the blue sky. An occasional cloud drifted across the pattern, and somewhere a long ways away, people were laughing. Six inches from my right hand, I noticed that a tiny lizard stood immobile, gazing at me, before darting up a tree, its color hiding it immediately. A hot, lazy day, and, for once, I was relatively at peace—for how long, I didn't know, but I was enjoying it. If only it could just stay like this . . .

But my mind would not stay still. The thought came sliding in starting up the old monotonous pattern. What a shame to have to go back to the city in such a short time, just when Jean is beginning to have some fun, I thought, having glanced at them playing in the water far out in the lagoon. I tried to stop the thought right there, but it was too late.

Back to the city—back to what? I don't even know what I'm going to do. The anxiety rose up again, only this time it brought with it a brand new thought. It was less than a thought, merely the faintest hint of a suggestion. "Why can't you go back? Why not try again? You are rested now; your mind will be creative, you will come up with ideas that will revolutionize the church and bring people to Christ. You've been depressed before and you've always snapped out of it. That's all this is, just a minor depression. Don't the people want you back? Come on, pull yourself together and go back."

I rolled over and buried my head in my hands in the hot sand. No, maybe that would have worked in the past, but not this time. This time I knew I was finished. This time I had seen myself. And after that, there was no more tolerance for self-deception.

The cry of a gull caught my attention, and I turned to see if I could spot it. It was circling lazily, higher and higher, riding an invisible current for its lift. I tried to imagine what I might look like through its eyes—a tiny figure under the palms. Was that what I looked like to God? No! God knew every hair on my head. He knew every cell in my body, and every atom in every cell. He knew everything that had ever happened to me, every thought or feeling I had ever had. And He not only knew, He *loved* me with a love so perfect, it was far beyond my human comprehension. A love I had never deserved and had never earned, that had held me when I deserved to be dropped.

"Then *why* Father?" I cried aloud. "Why have You let me down? You *know* I have tried and tried until I can try no more. I have exhausted all the creativeness of my brain. I have done every single thing I know how to do to serve You and build Your church, and it's all come to nothing. Zero! Even if I had another idea, I wouldn't trust it. No, Lord, I have had it. I can't do it. I mean it, and I am not going back on what I'm saying . . ."

Then He spoke. Clearly. Words that broke through all the torment tumbling around inside of me. Words that stopped my prayer in mid-air. Words that contained such a blast of revelation that my life would never be the same again.

At last you have seen it. You cannot do it. I have never asked you to do it. I, only I, can build My church. Will you stand aside, and let Me build it through you?

In that moment, a shaft of light poured into my soul, a light that dispelled all darkness, and took away all blindness. In an instant, I saw clearly.

The light of that simple truth continued to build within me until it was like a mighty river that swept through my whole being. And it carved a channel within that was totally new. A river that pulled down dead trees and tore up the underbrush of years, and bore it away on its current. A mighty torrent that picked up even boulders and tossed them aside, revealing God's truth beneath.

In that moment of eternity, the light bathed every area of my life, and set me free. It illuminated every question I had—and answered them all.

Now I could see it! It was all as clear as day. The Sun of Righteousness had risen with healing in His wings.

I leaned back on my elbows, stunned and excited, like a man who has stumbled on an enormous treasure and gradually realizes that he will never have to work—or worry—again. Dumb wonder—for the treasure had been right in his very backyard, walked over, sat on, even lectured on, but never discovered until this miraculous moment.

From deep within, a chuckle began—a laugh from the core of my spirit. And I realized that I hadn't laughed for months. Now, the joy of the Lord began from deep within.

Oh, the glorious simplicity and depth of this! Of course He alone could build His church. What a proud, arrogant fool I had been to even try to do it. How foolish that I should set about it with the techniques of men.

His work! Who else?

Suddenly, all nature seemed to be alive around me, and I was seeing it for the first time. The intricate beauty of the palm fronds—the marvel of the trunk. The wonder of the sinuous vines that trailed from the trees. All reflected the Glory of the Creator, even the lizard who had disappeared into his background. Oh God! How great You are! Shall I assist You in creation? Shall I help You make a world? Shall I instruct You on the molecular structure of a grain of sand? How much less do You need help in building Your church! Father, forgive me. Forgive my ridiculous presumption.

All these years *I* had been trying to build the church. Of course, I had failed. Thank You, Lord, that I *did* fail—that I could so clearly see You as the All in All. Otherwise, I actually might have thought that I had something to do with it.

In this light, I now could understand how we had *ever* known that vibrant presence of the Living God: it happened on the rare occasions that we had stepped out of His way—almost without realizing it.

To think that I had paid lip service to this truth for years—yet never really known it. Now, in that one word from God that had invaded my whole being, I saw God in His Awesome Power and Majesty. All my own efforts at working for God, lay in heaps of broken pieces. An insult to such Majesty. Before His glory, all I could do was praise, worship, and laugh for joy. Could I create the orchid that hung from the bush? Could I make the sun rise over the lagoon tomorrow morning? Could I make the sea return to its place? No! Not any more than I could bring about the spiritual birth of a soul. Nor could I produce a company of people who were united in Jesus. It was His work—and His alone.

Insight upon insight was pouring in upon me, and I was afraid of missing something. It came in blinding clarity concerning living the Christian life. This was an area that I had seen and rejoiced in for years—that Christianity was Christ living in me. The last couple of years had dulled it, but now, I saw afresh my own salvation as being all in Him. I could only present myself on the basis of what Jesus had done—the work was all His.

Being involved in His work was the same. My only part was submission to Him, and yieldedness. He would use me when and where and how He chose. I was to be directed by Him, to be no more than a tool in His hands. A clear channel for Him to flow through.

Only a channel. How many times had I sung that in hymns and songs. How many sermons had I actually preached around it—without ever seeing the totality of that statement. Not just me, getting a boost from Him, to do His work—but Him doing His work, and me borne along in His strength. The initiative, the idea, the direction, the empowering—and sustaining—strength all flowing from Him. Like a piece of wood borne on a stream—no struggle involved, just carried and directed in a force beyond itself. The force of the entire river behind it.

A sea gull soared and wheeled overhead. Suddenly my spirit was with that bird, high in God's heavens. As it hardly moved a feather, but submitted to the air currents—so I was borne by the invisible spirit, without any struggle of myself.

I let out a hallelujah as I saw the rest of what was already mine in God and just waiting to be claimed. Not by trying, or struggling to accomplish—but just learning to follow the direction of the Spirit, and be borne by Him to heights and accomplishments beyond myself.

I asked His forgiveness for all my pride over the years, for the slick professionalism which had taken the place of the Holy Spirit. I praised Him for every heartbreaking, heart-rending event of the past year. I praised Him for every detail that had finally broken me. I praised Him for the real death to self that He had worked in me, to the point where all confidence in myself had been broken.

The Holy Spirit seemed to draw my attention to the fact that we are only living stones. He must build us. A stone cannot build itself into a building—it must be taken and built by a builder. So I could not possibly achieve God's purpose in my life. He must achieve His own purpose; it seemed that He said, *Live in the passive voice. Do not struggle to do; let Me live and will through you.*

I had been doing the living. I had grabbed a promise of God, and tried to make it happen. I had gritted my teeth to obey and go through with it. Now I saw that God was *All.* Not just the Promise, but all the rest of it as well. My only contribution could be yieldedness, submission. *Choosing* to let Him *be* the All in All.

I shook my head, scooped up a handful of sand and let it sift through my fingers. I had been so foolish— Happy shouts came from the water's edge. Jean came running up, a towel flying in the wind. "It's dinnertime, and there's a bus waiting for us!" she announced breathlessly.

She stopped and looked at me curiously. "Got anywhere?" Something must have been showing. She slipped a dress on over her swimsuit—looking at me expectantly.

Got anywhere! I had been to heaven and back. I had soared in the heavenlies. I had seen the Holy One. I, who was dead, was alive with Another Life. I had heard Jesus. I had seen Him as All in All, not needing any puny efforts of my struggling service, but able to build His own church, using me when He chose to, where He chose to, how He chose to. The immense burden had been removed, rolled away. A new river had carved its way through my soul. I felt like shouting for all to hear, "It's His work, not mine." I was a man in harmony. All the pieces had fallen into place. The jigsaw was together.

But instead of shouting, nothing came out. The words froze in my throat.

A paralyzing thought invaded me: Wait till you get back to the city, and then see what happens. Take another look at the congregation, and then see what you feel! You'll be back in the same old despair, soon enough. Are you going to break Jean's heart again by saying that you have the answers? Better wait until you can prove it.

The glowing testimony dribbled over my lips half-heartedly. "I think we'll be going back to the city."

But inside I was still overwhelmed with what I had seen, still delighting with an inexpressible joy.

As we headed for the hotel bus, the hot-dog stand sent out its Coney Island odors to greet us, and I praised God. The radio was blaring, "O come all ye faithful . . ."

It didn't sound offensive at all. It was music from heaven, and angels couldn't have sung better. My heart joined in the chorus: "O come let us adore Him, O come let us adore Him, O come let us adore Him, Christ the Lord. . . ."

We boarded the bus, and I continued singing inside—going on into a chorus that we sang to the same tune: "For He alone is worthy, For He alone is worthy, For He alone is worthy, Christ the Lord. . . ."

6

The next day dawned clear and beautiful, and my spirit was still dancing for joy within. Again we headed for the beach. I had not felt excitement like this since the night I had received the Baptism in my boyhood. As we walked to the beach, my feet felt a message from my spirit, and it was all I could do to keep from dancing for sheer joy.

My Bible was in my duffel bag, and I sensed the Presence of the Holy Spirit more powerfully than I ever had before. By grace unfathomed, I had discovered a relationship to Him that was total, and I knew that He was now my Teacher, in a way that I had never known before. When we got to the beach, I was going to sit down with Him, and He was going to show me from the Bible, exactly what kind of relationship that was. I had always been skeptical of experiences that just hung by themselves, with no scriptural foundation.

Turn Your Back on the Problem

We usually took the bus to the beach, but this morning was so glorious within and without, we had to walk. The trees on both sides of the road met overhead, wrapping us in soft shadows and vines hung like streamers of confetti down to the road. Lizards stood immobile, looking at us sideways from their large eyes—before darting into the underbrush at the side of the road. Birds sang and chattered in every tree. In places where the trees thinned, the sunlight made a dappled pattern on the road, giving us a golden carpet to walk on. The whole world seemed to be alive with the glory of God.

Jesus Christ was All in All. I had known that He was my only hope in salvation, and my All in so many ways. Now I knew He was All in *all* things—including the ministry. What peace! No wonder I felt like dancing. The words of Jesus meant more than ever now: "My yoke is easy, my burden is light."

Again I tried to share what was happening with Jean, but for the life of me, I could not verbalize what had transpired. But somehow, she had sensed what was going on, and was content to wait until it was ready to be shared. Nor was it that difficult to discern. Whereas before, I must have been nearly knocking people over with my negative attitude, now I could almost feel the joy exuding from the pores of my skin. And I sensed that Jean was rejoicing with me, and for me.

It would be easier to talk when I knew from the Bible what had happened to me. But this much I already knew: I had rediscovered the Holy Spirit. Me! A Pentecostal of seventeen years standing! And I revered Him. He was Absolute Lord and Master. I could never again see Him as just power for service, to be used when needed. Now, He would use me, and do with me as He pleased. I was a feather borne in His powerful breeze—a chip of wood swept on His rushing current. But primarily, I saw Him as Teacher, Director of my spiritual life. And I was His hungry pupil, His disciple.

We sat under the palms again. Jean had a book and was sunbathing. I sat motionless, my spirit waiting.

First, He took me to the life of Moses in the Old Testament—and showed me the unbelievable similarities between my experience and that of Moses. In so many heartbreaking ways our lives had run parallel. Moses knew the Living God, and made some costly decisions in the light of what he knew. Because of seeing the Invisible God, he had refused the hedonistic Egyptian way of life. The Bible assured me that he did this by faith. His life was committed to the Invisible God.

Moses had a call from God to deliver Israel, a call that gripped him and burned in his mind, and compelled him to visit with his enslaved brothers. It was at this point that he went wrong. *He tried to fulfill that call in his own natural ability.* He went wrong and stayed wrong for forty years. Had Moses been less talented, he might not have fallen into the trap. The trouble was, he had so much natural ability that he tried to use it for God, and when he did so, he got in the way and was not able to rest only in God and His Spirit.

It took a long time for this natural ability to be broken. Anything that Moses did to bring about the release of the people of Israel before he met God at the burning bush, could have been done without prayer and without supernatural empowering of the Holy Spirit. All he did had been learned in the Soldier School of Egypt,

59

and it smelt of the academics that he had been through. It was Moses trying to do God's work. It was Moses doing a work for God.

But God's work bears the stamp of God. It cannot be achieved by man. It just ceases to be, if we eliminate prayer, waiting on God—and the Holy Spirit. God's work originates with Him, flows from Him, is accomplished in the power He provides and returns back to Him—giving Him all the glory.

Moses struggled to achieve God's purpose, and God allowed him to fail—He had to! It was a vital part of his spiritual education.

This was me! This had been the bent of my life these many years, struggling to emulate what I saw on the pages of the Bible. I had not fully realized that the One who spoke that Bible, is the only One who can achieve it in this generation. All of my imagination, my creativeness—all of my own natural abilities in communicating had been poured out, and God had allowed me to walk into failure to bring me to utter helplessness. He had to, because, with my enormous pride, I never would have listened otherwise. I *had to be* smashed flat, without hope. Thank You, Lord, for every one of the failures.

I moved my feet in the hot sand and felt every footstep of Moses as he went across the desert. I gripped his staff and plodded with him. The blowing sand stung our faces. That desert became the Lord's blast furnace. A burning caldron of truth in which all pretense and self-deception were boiled away, leaving only the pure metal behind. My seared and scorched mind went with Moses through the shame and frustration, defeat and failure, the fear of the past and the future. From deep within, the awful cry, "I have let God down." A call from God that I couldn't fulfill, now lay shattered in the dust.

A hundred failures had brought me to that place. I walked the barren slopes of Sinai with Moses as we tended our flocks. The oppressive silence, the endless re-playing of past events. The sense that God had left us. Never realizing that in those brooding silences and moments of despair, the breaking was taking place, the death that was mine with Jesus at the Cross was now being test-probed into my very being by the Holy Spirit. It was no phony death; it was real and dark.

Those Virgin Islands had become my Golgotha.

Moses! How we tried to work for God! How I made *my* plans, and asked the Lord to bless them. How I had gone ahead, assuming that I had the Holy Spirit working with me. Yet I had been so full of myself as I threshed around in my earnest endeavors and grand ideas that I hadn't even noticed the strange absence of His Presence. Thank You, Lord, for loving me enough to send me to Brooklyn, there to really face myself.

Then a broken and defeated Moses, in despair and haunted by fear, was suddenly blasted with a revelation of God in His all sufficiency. God who said His name was the I Am, dumb-founded him. The bush burned with God's glory and Moses fell worshiping before Him. He now had his back to the needs of Israel in Egypt. He had no confidence left in himself, no possible hope of deliverance from his own creative ability as a source. His entire dependence was upon God—whose name was I Am.

Then God said, "I will come down and deliver ... go thou ... "

Turn Your Back on the Problem

I re-lived the experience of yesterday. How many times had I read this verse, and not really heard what it was saying? Now it had happened to me. The Holy Spirit, my Teacher, moved my eyes across the words. God alone could deliver and build His church of that day, and Moses, at last, broke, and as wet clay, was now to be formed into a mighty tool in God's hand, and a mouth for Him to speak through.

When Moses returned to Egypt, not one thing could have taken place without prayer, waiting on God, and the empowering of the Holy Spirit. Every plan, every action, every word spoken originated with God—and was shown to Moses as he waited upon God. Moses was carried in the flow of the Living God. The God who was ever there, gently making His Presence, Mind, and Purpose known to those who had the ears to hear. God was the Prime Mover, and Moses did as he was instructed. God, the Invisible Director—Moses, the obedient directed one. God spoke the words, and Moses merely repeated them to the people.

Despite the warmth of the beach, my flesh chilled. Could this really be? Could it really work out in a church in Brooklyn? If it could ... what a new view of the ministry, of the church and of every facet of church life! Fantastic! Unbelievable! Yet even as my mind reeled under the possibility, I knew the Holy Spirit was making it come alive in my heart. This is how He would build His church—it would be His work; whatever part I was to play would be given me step by step.

I got up from the beach blanket. "I think I'll go for a walk, honey." Jean just smiled under her sun hat, and understood. In less than a minute I was again the student, eagerly awaiting the next lesson.

The whole thing was almost too much, entirely out of the realm of theory and professionalism. The Holy Spirit, the Teacher, was really speaking, directing and acting today. Was I dreaming this, imagining it? No! If anything, He was making this almost too real as He fitted the jigsaw of my life together.

I was walking down the beach toward a distant, deserted cove. The waves rolled over my feet, the wet sand oozed between my toes. Quietly I praised God in my worship language, feeling as free and excited as a child. What a purpose to life! What fullness! No longer struggling to make life and service happen—but the Holy Spirit directing, instructing and pointing the way.

No longer could the white ceiling of my hotel room condemn me with its emptiness. The future was now a container of the Living God! Every detail, every opportunity, every test, every hour, every moment was made for Him to express Himself through, to execute His own purpose—and to use me in any way He chose.

Two couples were having a picnic on the beach, and they looked up to watch me as I went by. I suddenly realized that I was bursting with this unbelievable horizon that was unfolding within. I was gazing at the waves, the trees, the flowers, everything with a new awe and joy, seeing reflections of God in all, and I guess it showed enough for these people to stop in mid-sandwich to look at me. I grinned and hurried on my way.

People that a few days ago had irritated me I now saw as those with whom the Holy Spirit was working to lead them to Jesus. People that before had made me afraid, because I couldn't share Jesus effectively, I could now love freely, because I knew He was doing the sharing, and I was just the witness. How can that love that wells up within and reaches out to anonymous people, faces in the crowd, be explained? I knew a wondrous freedom to love as I walked along that crowded beach.

Gradually, the crowd thinned, until I was alone. At the end of the bay was a pile of boulders—occupied only by a few lizards and birds. In the shadow of these rocks I sat and worshiped Him who in grace had brought me this far.

My Teacher led my mind back to the Acts of the Apostles. A few days ago, these strange, confident men had made me both afraid and angry. Now, I felt akin to them—I had the answers now, and almost fellowshiped with them.

It was so obvious: the disciples had not initiated the events in Jerusalem surrounding the Day of Pentecost, God had. They were involved, but God did it. All they did was worship God, and they were spontaneously led by the Holy Spirit, into an evangelistic happening.

Nor had Philip initiated a revival in Samaria. He proclaimed the Good News, but the results were far greater than he ever could have achieved with natural talent. He was directed there by the Holy Spirit.

His stay was terminated by the Holy Spirit, as He directed him to speak to the Ethiopian. What incredible planning by the Omniscient Spirit! The Ethiopian was reading from exactly the right verse in Isaiah, and Philip was directed alongside at exactly the right moment. It was beyond all human comprehension—and the Holy Spirit had achieved it all, using Philip whose only act was to respond at once in blind obedience to the prompting of the Holy Spirit.

Turn Your Back on the Problem

Before, I had looked at Philip in anger. How come he always seemed to know where and when to be? I hated feeling so left out, while these men seemed to share some great secret they were almost deliberately keeping from me. Now we smiled at each other through the pages. I knew the secret. It was not what they had, it was *Who had them.* Their secret was in their Director, and I had missed Him only because I was too self-sufficient to acknowledge my great need of Him at every step.

The other character who visited with me, now so real in the pages of Acts, was Ananias, of Damascus. He was just an ordinary disciple, but did he go knocking at every door in Damascus, searching for the right man to speak with? No! There it was again—the unseen, Omniscient Director, giving all the orders. He brought about the happenings. It was His work. Ananias was directed to the street and the house, where he found a seeking man. Ananias' sole contribution was obedience. But it was obedience of an unusual degree; unquestioning and instantaneous, not having to know why or how or who, not having to know anything, save that it was God doing the directing. And not having to finish dinner first or run an errand on the way, but going straightaway to do as directed.

Peter—worshiping and praying on the housetop, where he was taught, directed, and sent by the Holy Spirit to the house of Cornelius, to discover a prepared congregation—prepared by the Holy Spirit.

The early Christians did not make a move without constant reference to the Holy Spirit, who glorified Jesus, and made Him real and precious to the saints, and communicated Him to the world—through the mouths of attentive disciples. Their power was not some dynamic explosion—but rather a natural outcome of their walking in practical harmony with the Spirit who counseled them. Their power lay more in the quality of their obedience and their ability to hear Him tell them where to be, who to be talking to, and what to say—the explosive element was a natural after that.

Paul and Barnabas walked with sublime confidence across the Roman world. That confidence had frustrated me. I beat my fists against their history, because I didn't know where their confidence came from. Now it seemed to spring from every page. They were sent forth by the Holy Spirit from Antioch, and their story gives hints at the secret—"The Spirit suffered them not" and "Forbidden by the Spirit."

He was in them, His hand upon them. And they knew it. He walked them into myriad situations, and continually achieved His end. They *always* saw Him. Even in jail, they could praise God at the top of their voices, because they knew He was still Director and still achieving His ends. From Roman prison, Paul triumphantly affirms that he is the prisoner *of Jesus Christ.* He has been put there by the Director of All—to glorify God.

The Holy Spirit was not just power for service, to be on hand after man had used his brain to plan and contrive. *He* was the Director, the Planner—God Himself, using me at His own will. *This* is what the Baptism in the Holy Spirit was all about.

All these years as a Spirit-filled Christian, I had enjoyed as much as I saw. I had thrilled to the new realm in prayer and worship. The way He had released me from bondage, and the ability I had known in sharing Christ, without any question, He *had* used me over the years. But this was a new horizon—something I could have known so long ago, but through arrogant blindness had missed.

Suddenly all was still. Though it was early afternoon, I was enveloped by the stillness of twilight. I sensed that He had taught all I was to learn today. The excitement and intent listening was over; I relaxed in the glory of what I had seen.

What else could I do but bow my head and make a re-dedication of myself to Him who was in me, and upon me. I was His, to do whatever He wanted.

As I got up and headed back, the whole beach seemed alive with Him. I walked slowly and softly—almost afraid to disturb the Presence.

Jean sat under a palm tree, reading. "Honey . . ." I was glowing inside, but again it wouldn't come out. One minute of revelation makes everything so clear, but takes hours to explain. In fact, when it is put into words, it doesn't seem so much after all—it is what has been *seen* that is so transforming.

"Honey, we are going back to the city. I have been getting in the way, and now I am going to relax and let God do His work—anyway He wants." It sounded so ridiculously weak. It was but the faintest echo of what was a torrent seeking for a way out from deep within.

But the weak words had communicated. She looked up and positively beamed, "I'm so glad you're happy. I knew God would speak to you."

That night, after days of perfect weather, it started to rain again—buckets, just as it had the day we arrived. After two more solid days, we cut our vacation short and headed back to Brooklyn.

7

Tired, sunburned, travel-weary passengers poured from planes, pushing their way toward the immigration desks, bags and packages and cameras slung from shoulders and clutched in aching arms. A man with a packet from India, another from the Orient. A little businessman who had obviously been through all this many times before, waited in resignation. A fat man, trying to convince himself of his importance, blew cigar smoke into our eyes, and cursed everyone within earshot.

We were in the International Arrivals Building at Kennedy Airport, inching our way towards customs. Nerves and tempers were frayed, until the atmosphere seemed ready to explode.

I slipped out of the crowd into a telephone booth, to call Floyd. They were not expecting us yet. I dialed our home number, and heard Floyd's familiar voice at the other end.

"Floyd, it's Malcolm! We're back, and stranded at Kennedy—any chance of your coming and getting us?"

"You're home!" He could not hide the shock in his voice. "I'll be right over. What happened?"

"We got washed out—we'll be at the entrance doors of the International Arrivals Building."

Soon through customs, we walked toward the swinging doors that would take us back to the city. I looked up at the hundreds of people staring down at us through a glass balcony—searching for arriving friends. We felt like fish in a tank in a pet-store window. Something made me recall the first time I had looked up to that balcony—and seen Pastor E. C. Erikson and David Kyvik, scanning the crowd for me. What a lot had happened since then!

We made our way through the crowds milling in the foyer of the building—finding a place near the door. Jean sat on our suitcases, while I stood at the door watching for Floyd's car.

Outside it was December dark, cold, and drizzling, a miserable, polluted mist. We were back.

But I felt another atmosphere—an atmosphere I always feel in the city. The spiritual atmosphere was polluted to the point where it could be felt, and that night the air seemed to be alive with the millions of empty futile lives that were within a thirty-mile radius, heavy and thick with hate, and greed, and selfishness. I seemed to hear and feel the oppression of it all. It seemed I heard and felt the cries of thousands of addicts and the moan of empty, dead religion was on the air. This was death, spiritual death. I felt like saying as they had said of Lazarus, "Behold Lord, by now he stinketh."

Floyd pulled to the curbside, and while he spoke with

70

a policeman, we ran out of the building and were pulling away from the curb in moments.

"Welcome home! We are all waiting for you." I smiled weakly, inwardly praising God for Floyd, a brother in the work.

From Nebraska originally, he had come to work with me a few months previously with his wife, Judy, from Wisconsin, after lecturing and working in Chicago at Bible school. From the wheatfields of the Midwest, they had come to the concrete and asphalt of the East—and it was an instant marriage. Floyd and Judy fit into their new surroundings as if they were born for the job. He had already learned to love the people, and had taken over the church ably while I was away—but never trying to be more than an assistant.

We were soon out of the airport, and driving along the Belt Parkway. The drizzling rain made the roads slick, and an orchestra of horns and frustration moved us toward the city.

"How are the children?" Jean asked eagerly. We didn't leave them often, and they had been deeply missed.

"Oh, they're great! Karen missed you at bedtime, but apart from that, everything was beautiful."

"And the dog?" Our little French poodle. "That dog!" Floyd showed disgust. "Walking him every night is for the birds. It's insanity in this weather." And we all laughed—everything was fine on the domestic scene.

"How has the church been?"

Floyd was serious now. "Well, we have never had so many people out to the prayer meetings. Needless to say, everyone has been praying that you would come back. Apart from that, I guess everything is about the same."

He went on to detail specific problems with certain people, and developments in others. Things were about the same.

The conversation lulled as Floyd searched for a break in the traffic to get into a line that was moving. The posted speed limit smiled mockingly down at us, 55 MPH. That was a laugh—fifteen miles an hour would have been appreciated at that point.

The side of the parkway was in the usual con-dition—except that the trash was soggy now. An aban-doned auto was being stripped and demolished by a gang of teenagers. New York was the same, and the church was the same.

A voice seemed to whisper in my ear: "And you are the same. Nothing has changed since you left."

I felt suddenly weak and helpless, and the old fear which I had actually forgotten about began to gnaw at my vitals like a starving rat. How could I withdraw the resignation? Nothing was different, including the creeping, bumper-to-bumper traffic. I felt I was sinking fast, about to drown in a black swamp of despair.

Desperately, I groped for a memory. If only I could feel as I had felt on the beach in the Virgin Islands. Please, Father, let me feel it again. Let me know that You are going to build Your church here.

We were passing a jungle of apartment houses. They towered above us in the night, all around us. Millions of tiny lights blinked and flickered through the mist and rain. Who could ever get inside those buildings and share Christ? Everyone was so afraid in this city; they would never open the door to their homes, or their hearts. The apartments glowered down, impregnable fortresses. The rat was joined by others.

Turn Your Back on the Problem

My waking nightmare was broken by Floyd's question, "Well, what have you decided? Are you coming back?"

I was nearly under, but with some kind of last reserve, I clung to what I knew the Holy Spirit had become to me, and had shown me. Yet, the rats were hard at it. "I think we are coming back—but I don't know yet."

It was nearly Christmas, and we were pushed immediately into the next rush, buying presents, and preparing for the holidays in the short time left. There was little preaching and plenty of time to take another look at the revelation He had given me—this time from the cold asphalt pavements, rather than a beach in the Virgin Islands.

In the middle of Christmas week, there was a call from Roy Johnson, pastor of the Philadelphia Church in Seattle. We had been close friends for a number of years, and I went regularly to his church to minister.

His voice was happy and expectant. "So we'll see you on Sunday, and I just wanted to know what time your flight gets in."

My mind groped for what he was talking about. In the chaos of the last weeks, I hadn't even looked at my date-book, or thought of engagements to preach. I reached for my calendar and flipped it to the New Year.

Sure enough, I was scheduled for a crusade in Seattle, with lectures to the Bible students every morning, but I had it down for the second and third weeks of January. Not only had I forgotten it, but we had crossed lines at the time of the booking. Roy was expecting me in Seattle in four days.

Turn Your Back on the Problem

I hurriedly explained the situation and was about to put him off, until the decisions I faced were resolved. It was then that I heard the whisper of the Holy Spirit. "Go to Seattle when he wants you."

"Roy? Forget what I just said. I'll be there, if I can get a flight."

If I could get a flight! Impossible. Every flight out of the city was jammed for the New Year holidays, had been booked for weeks, with waiting lists closed. I called airline after airline and tried every possible route—and drew a blank. But a curious thing happened: the more hopeless the situation became, the more I found myself becoming encouraged and excited. I *knew* I would get out to the west coast, and I *knew* that this was a vital part of the plan of God for me. I instinctively knew that this was the last part of what God had to show me.

Finally, every airline had been contacted, every conceivable connection had been tried, and there was no way to Seattle. I had even tried to go via Alaska—but every seat to every place out of the city was reserved.

"Father, I know You want me to go, and I know that all things are possible for You. I'm going to turn my back on this and let You work it out." And I picked up the phone and called TWA one more time. "You've got to get me to Seattle—by any route."

"Well, just a minute." There was a pause and a whirring clatter of a computer. "We have just received a cancellation on flight number 483 to San Francisco—and we can put you up the coast to Seattle." It was unbelievable, and I praised God, as my expectation mounted. I would miss the first meeting—but apart from that, I would be on schedule.

Back again at Kennedy Airport, I edged my way to

the ticket counter. It seemed that every collegian in New York was going skiing in the west. They sat on their duffel bags, carrying skis on their shoulders, and talked of their life. I stood among them, and listened. It was a familiar story of drugs, acid trips, sex parties, hate of parents, rebellion at authorities—and general irresponsibility. Was there any way of reaching these long-haired kids, with hearts so wide open? They had tried everything. These kids knew, categorically, that nothing in the world satisfied. They had seen the emptiness of their parents' faith in affluence. Their faded blue jeans cried out their disgust at a phony plastic society which lived behind a front as it worshiped at the shrine of possessions. Rejecting that, they plunged into their own brand of freedom—freedom from all restraints. Now, their empty, bored eyes said all too clearly that they knew the answer was not here either. Would I ever be able to communicate Jesus to such as these? I sensed that what the Holy Spirit would say to me now would give me the answers—all of them. The mammoth 747 loomed outside the building, and with high anticipation I made my way to my seat. The Holy Spirit was going to show me something more, and I *knew* a final decision would be reached.

As I sat down in my seat, I pulled out my yellow pad and Bible—and waited. It was the first time that I had ever been on a 747, but my eyes never saw the details. Nor did I hear the bustle of the passengers, the modulated announcements of the stewardesses, the roar of the accelerating engines. All my concentration was on what would be communicated in the depths of my innermost being.

Then, in a rush it came. A final understanding of all

that He had been saying to me. In a flash, I saw my whole ministry—the mistakes, the failures, the heartbreaks—all from *His* point of view. The tangle of events suddenly fell into place. It was like looking at the stars. At first glance, they seem to be a jumble, thrown together by chance—but when an astronomer sits beside us, he shows us that there is a perfect pattern, an exact timing, and wonderful harmony. Stars so far away that they could not be seen with the naked eye have a great effect on this planet, lifting and pulling it as they pass. The Holy Spirit showed the telling details of my life—some so far away, so minute that, but for His touch, I would not have remembered. Events out at the edge of the galaxy of memory—each was a part of a perfect plan, each had a purpose, bringing me to this present moment. I saw the people who had come into my life, each one sent for reason—guiding, challenging, testing, holding me to the course He had planned.

I saw the mistakes, the failures and sins—the great guilt that yet lay deep within, accusing . . . He gave me not only a new appreciation for the Blood of Jesus that cleanses from all sin, but showed me that even my worst mistakes worked in His great plan. He could make the wrath and foolishness of man to praise Him. My most hideous mistakes were used to bring me much-needed humbling.

I wrote down what He showed me. The lectures for the students took shape. For I also saw what these aspirants to the ministry could be saved from. As the great jetliner soared above the clouds, my spirit soared to God—praising Him for His great goodness to me. Worshiping Him who Alpha and Omega, holding everything in His hands, directing even our mistakes into His will. Effortlessly we flew across the continent, and I sat praying, listening, and waiting.

Changing planes in San Francisco, I was still in the classroom, hardly aware of what was happening. I sat in the terminal building, writing away, stopped to board the next plane, got seated and wrote some more. Finally, as we prepared for landing in Sea-Tac Airport, I had my answer. The guidance was clear and strong, only it was based wholly on God's word over the past weeks. I could not yet leave New York City. I was to return in total dependence upon the Holy Spirit, get out of the way and watch Him work.

Seattle was where Carroll and Vivian Forseth lived, and we loved to go there, just to see them. It was Carroll who met me at the airport and took me into Seattle. Usually we would sit up till all hours of the night, talking over old crusades we had shared together, and planning for possible crusades in the future. But this time, I quietly mentioned that I had seen God in such a new way that I would never be the same again. We sat for hours during the next few days, sharing these concepts.

The next morning, I stood before the student body of the Seattle Bible Training School, and introduced what I was going to share with them.

"Many students leave a school like this with big ideas, big plans for the future, all the great things that they are going to do for God. But the hard truth is—and you had better hear it now—that a shocking number fall by the wayside. And even more live in quiet frustration all their lives, not accomplishing one-tenth of what they dreamed of. In these lectures, I am going to share with you what it has taken me seventeen years to finally learn concerning the ministry of the Holy Spirit, and I am still learning. I will say just one more thing before we begin: not one of you is going to do a single thing for God. Either *He* does the doing, or it doesn't get done . . ." And with that, the Holy Spirit, through me, launched into a biblical explanation of what He had shown me.

I was a new man, and I knew it. I was ready to return to Brooklyn, and let Him build His church through me.

8

It was the evening of the last Friday in January, 1971. The annual business meeting of the church attended by most of the congregation was in progress, in the basement of Salem Gospel Tabernacle. We had eaten a fellowship meal and had listened to the reports from every department of the church. At the table at the head of the room, I sat with my assistant and associates, and their wives—Floyd and Judy Nicholson, of course, and Brian and Nancy Hughes, who were pioneering a branch work in Florham Park, New Jersey, and Tom and Connie Hatcher, who were pioneering a branch work to the north of the city. We had long had excellent fellowship, and over the last weeks my heart had ached because of the effects my decision would have on their lives.

My words to the meeting were scheduled for the end of the meeting, and it was at this time that I was to announce to them my future intentions. Most had heard something of what I had shared with one or two about what had happened in the Islands, but no one knew for sure.

The clock ticked on to 10:30 P.M., and the last fiscal report was finished. I fingered the letter that I was going to read to them. What an eternity stood between this letter and the one I had read in this basement only a few short weeks before! I had entered into death and had known a glorious resurrection.

Would I ever be able to communicate what had happened to me? Or would it come across as just so many words and clichés? I rose to my feet and began to read. Briefly, I outlined the events that had led up to the revelation of God in the Virgin Islands, and continued, "I will return to be your pastor, on the condition that everyone understands that I can do nothing. I am completely unable to lead you to be the kind of church we know must be. I have realized that the Holy Spirit is the Director, and knowing that I cannot do it, I am handing this church over to Him to do whatever He has to do."

With a few words of exhortation to all, as I came to the end of my letter, a holy hush fell over the gathering. Then praise began to ascend to God from all over the basement. Tom Hatcher broke down. God showed him to stop trying and let God be God that night. We closed the meeting around one hour later praising God.

I was the pastor of Salem again, with a new sense of extraordinary anticipation. I was about to behold the Holy Spirit at work.

The next morning, I went to my office and closed the

door behind me. The books on the shelves were the same. The desk, tidy now, was the same. The valentine still stuck out behind the filing cabinet. But *I* was totally different.

What should I do now? How does a man let the Holy Spirit run the church? I had *said* that the Holy Spirit would be in control—but how was this going to work out in actual hour-by-hour practice? A few weeks ago I would have gone across the room, sat at the desk, and after a brief prayer, begun to plan and work out a schedule and program aimed at bringing people into the church. I knew I could never do it like that again.

I looked at the green swivel chair behind my desk. From that chair had originated my plans, plans I now saw to be human, many of them untouched by God. I went over to the chair, but instead of sitting in it, I knelt beside it, and began to pray.

"Father, thank You for what you have shown me. Thank You for everything that has brought me to this moment. Thank You for the breaking of my heart. I don't know where to go from here, but one thing I do know; this chair is Yours! You are running this church. I am going to listen to You, and this is Your Director's chair."

It sounded ridiculous. Certainly, He who is Spirit, filling all things, did not go to the chair—nor did He need this chair or any other chair. Never mind; I needed to say it, and something changed.

I went over to the files where I kept all the elaborate plans and programs that I had put so much trust in. I picked them out, and dropped them, one by one, into the wastebasket.

But still I did not know how to find His direction.

Turn Your Back on the Problem

How can a person be realistically led by the Spirit? On faith, I was renouncing one kind of action, the kind that originated in my intellect. Now how did I discover the actions that originated with Him?

Mere passivity was not the answer; in fact, sitting back with a blank, open mind was downright dangerous. That much I knew. The men of the Bible were men of action. That was putting it mildly. But their activity originated in God. It was not fretful, surging, self-exciting, self-generated energy. They were at peace in their hearts quietly waiting on God, and upon receiving His mind and will, they were obedient, carrying out His directions in His strength.

They were surrendered men. Surrendered to Him, on His terms, not theirs, to be led where and how He desired.

"How, Lord?" I whispered the question into the air that was alive with His Presence.

The needs and the problems that we faced as a church came to mind. The membership list was on the desk in front of me. I reached for it and read each family. Each one represented a problem, or a cry for a move of God. *"Needs!* Yes, I see them, but how do I know Your direction, what action You would initiate?" I questioned Him.

I recalled then that needs had been Moses' problem. He had gone to his Israelite brethren and tried to meet their needs, and had so hopelessly failed.

What did he do that met the needs? The Holy Spirit asked the question within me, like a gunshot. My answer was almost as spontaneous. "He turned his back on the problem, and worshiped God at the burning bush." *You must do the same,* came the immediate reply. Turn my back on the problem, and worship God! Yet at that moment it seemed so obvious. That was the very essence of faith in action.

Because I had finally seen that I really *could* do nothing, and had begun to see that He was the Everything and the All, I *could* turn my back and rest in Him. I could stop my fretting, fruitless actions and simply worship Him, who was now working out all things according to His purpose and plan.

Having caught a glimpse of Him in His majesty, I began to see Him, the Living, Invisible God now active in the affairs of men—particularly in Brooklyn, in Salem, and in me—I could now afford to stop all my works, and worship.

If He had declared that He was building His church, and if I believed that and saw it by faith, even in the most discouraging situations, then what else could I do *but* worship? Should I, in my puny wisdom, my limited knowledge, seek to advise the All-Knowing One on how to do His work? All I could do was to kneel before such a One and adore Him.

While I still had confidence in myself, it was natural to set out to meet the needs, to take pride in my ideas, to rely on my wisdom, talents and abilities. Now that was smashed and all that was left was Him—the All.

I began to understand. It was as Moses worshiped at the bush that he began to know from his heart, and his head, what God was about to do. In worship, God shared His thoughts with Moses. In worship, prostrate before God's Presence, he received orders that initiated action that rocked, and finally toppled Egypt. As he lay in awe before God, he received the words he was to say.

The action that God initiated in the lives of others started as Moses worshiped. People that Moses needed to help him in the work began to move toward him as he beheld and adored God.

Others, like Pharaoh, who set themselves against God's people, began to collapse. Impossible problems were solved—not as Moses set out with ideas to solve them, but as he waited on God, who Himself was the all-sufficient answer.

From the moment he fell before the bush and took off his shoes—humbled and awed by the God he beheld there—there flowed a river of power and faith to the world that gave it the Exodus.

Hardly aware of what I was doing, I began to quietly worship Him. I had always worshiped, and had done so vocally, with the new tongue He had given me at the time of my Baptism in the Holy Spirit—but this new worship came out of a heart that saw He was *All.* It was being spell-bound by God Himself.

My back was to the problems that so desperately needed an answer. He was the answer, and therefore I praised Him even though I couldn't see it.

Whatever, whoever, would communicate Jesus Christ to Brooklyn, only He knew. No human on earth could break through the hard shell that encased the people of Brooklyn—but He could, and I adored Him who is Love, Mercy and All Power.

In those moments I saw that He really was the Living God in this place. He was *here*, now, acting in sovereign love and power, bringing to pass His purpose. And I told Him what I saw, in praise.

Turn Your Back on the Problem

The Plan of Salvation was never so vivid. The perfect death of Jesus had taken sin away. His triumphant Resurrection, His authority in the Ascension, what could be added? Nothing. All that was now in the Person of Jesus made so real by the Spirit.

The Holy Spirit directed my mind back to a lesson I had learned, but had never really understood. Eighteen months before, I had taken our daughter Donna to our doctor for a checkup. It happened that I had a large wart on my back that had troubled me a little. It had changed its shape, and it had begun to leave blood spots on my shirt. Casually, I asked the doctor to look at it while Donna was dressing.

One look was enough. As I pulled my shirt back on, the doctor avoided my eyes.

"I can never be absolutely sure without a biopsy, but..." He hesitated for a moment, then looked up at me, his eyes saying more than the words that followed. "I am 99 percent certain that you have melanoma, the most lethal cancer there is. I am going to call Memorial Hospital right now to see how soon I can get you in."

I had read about the Sloan Kettering Memorial Hospital, on the east side of Manhattan, in *Reader's Digest*. It dealt only with cancer, and it was the best in the world. Thoughts vied for pre-eminence. Part of me said that it simply couldn't be. A fellow of thirty-one years of age couldn't have cancer. I hadn't smoked—surely, not *me* ... Other thoughts said that even if it was, it would be a minor piece of surgery, nothing but the removal of a wart, really.

I left the office, numbed, clutching a piece of paper with an appointment time written on it. The thought that it was not serious because it was so small, had vanished; melanoma was lethal, whatever size it started out. But my mind still refused to accept the full impact of it. It just couldn't be happening to me.

Sunday morning, I told the congregation the facts and called the elders of the church to anoint me with oil and pray for me. It was the only action I felt led to take. I believed in divine healing as part of God's gift to me.

After a preliminary examination, I was hospitalized at once. Then they began to find more. Lumps in my lymph glands. Finally, it began to get hold of me that this was not a novel I was reading. *This was me.* I knew about cancer in the lymph glands. I had visited many cases as a pastor, and watched them die horrible deaths.

Many specialists examined me, one after another, confirming what had already been found. One sat down with me on the bed. I looked him in the eyes. "Doctor, I'm a minister. I know my Lord, and I am ready to be with Him, if He calls me. So, level with me—what are my chances?"

He hesitated, wanting to encourage, but unable to lie. "With what we have found in you, your chances are about three percent—or they could be as high as forty percent. Maybe a miracle, who knows?" He looked at me with pleading eyes; what else was there to say?

It was the night before surgery that the full force of it all hit me. The nurses of Memorial Hospital were the most wonderful I had ever met. Many nights I would sit until late, visiting with them and talking of Jesus. But that night, a different nurse, who did not work on the floor I was on, came to visit. The other patients in the ward were already asleep, or reading. The large window beside the bed looked out on the high-rise buildings of the east side—thousands of little lights against black silhouettes.

This strange nurse came into my room, bent over me and looked me square in the eyes: "So you're a preacher?" I nodded, wondering what was coming next.

"Do you know that most people die in this ward?" Her mouth was curled in a half smile, half sneer.

I didn't know what to answer. I had had no idea that I was on some sort of death row.

She continued to talk. "I have seen many people die. In fact, I have seen them die with what you have . . . But I have never seen a preacher die. I have always wanted to see if they really believed what they preach. This is going to be interesting. What does it feel like to be dying, preacher?"

Stunned and numb, I licked lips that had become dry. As I answered, I was conscious of what I was saying, conscious of meaning it—but I had given no particular thought to it.

"Nurse, if it's death you're talking about, I'm not only ready, I am excited! If you were the Angel of Death telling me I was to die in five minutes, I would say let's go now. It's better than I have preached . . . But if it's a lingering death, with cancer in my glands, six months of rotting away . . . I'm sorry, but I'm human enough to be afraid. I don't want that." She smiled and left without a word.

I lay there with her words ringing in my ears. "What does it feel like to be dying, preacher?"

As I lay there, a male nurse came in to prepare me for surgery the next morning. As he shaved my back and chest, I realized how extensive the surgery was to be.

The surgeon had told me that if it was as they were sure it would be—I would have skin grafted from my leg, for the surgery on my back. In my mind, I could see it all.

Suddenly, terror rose within and screamed inside of me. "You prayed, and you weren't healed." The thoughts mocked me. Fear surged and receded like an ocean tide. And like the incoming tide, it always came closer, never withdrawing quite as far as before.

Suddenly, a thought came clearly through the tumultuous, encroaching fears: *You may not have been healed, but you have been promised the peace of God under all circumstances. Claim what is yours.*

I slipped out of my bed and went into the bathroom—the only place where I could be alone. I sank to my knees, and began to pray. And as I did, the greatness of God overwhelmed me.

It seemed that I saw myself as a cork on the ocean that was God. All Wisdom, All Love, All Power, limitless and unknown, beneath me, supporting me. I began to praise Him and worship Him. For some reason beyond me, but not beyond Him, I was here in this place, and though I didn't understand, I praised Him for what He was doing, even for the fact that I was kneeling on the cold tile floor. There was no pleading or begging; I did not need to plead with Him who loved me with a love that beggared description. All I could do in that moment was worship God for being Who He Was. Somehow, asking for healing at this point was so unimportant as to be forgotten. I was overwhelmed by the Healer Himself. I met Jesus then, as I had never met Him before. I worshiped Him in English, and I used the prayer language He had given me in the Baptism. And Heaven came down, and filled the room.

When I went back to bed, I fell asleep quietly, praising Him in other tongues. The word "cancer" had always been a fear-filled word, ugly and menacing—now, as I had worshiped Him, the word had lost its venom. It meant no more than "fried egg"—merely a word that described a condition.

The next morning when they came for me, I was so at peace on the ocean of His love, that I may have startled them. But I knew that He was in me, and I in Him forever. What else mattered?

As I came to consciousness in the recovery room, I had the vivid memory of the surgeon telling me that I would know if it had been cancer by my leg. In those foggy moments, I reached down to my leg to see if it was bandaged. It was swathed in bandages. I was acutely conscious of being held in love, even if I had cancer. I shouted, "Praise God!" and lapsed into unconsciousness.

Back in my room, the doctor told me that the wart had indeed been malignant. They had removed it, and had also taken out my lymph glands. He assured me that with radium treatment which would start in a few days, they had a good chance of arresting any further spread.

Two days later, the same doctor came back to tell me that analysis of the lymph glands had proved them to be free of cancer. Mistaken diagnosis. Almost never happens. You are in perfect health, and we need that bed— Go home!

Now I was in my study and the Holy Spirit was

vividly reminding me that without realizing what I was doing those months before, I had turned my back on the problem and worshiped God. He had then stepped in and accomplished His end. Now He had shown me this as a principle of life, and I knew that from here on, my back was to the needs and problems of Brooklyn, and I was engaged in worshiping Him.

9

During the days that followed, the Holy Spirit separated me into waiting in worship before God. This was very different for me. I, who had always been so intensely active, so very restless, was being stilled on the inside and taught to listen with patience. Not only had I never realized how restless I had been until the Spirit made me be still; I had never realized the nature of impatience. The fussy, pride-filled self-importance of it, and the utter distrust in God's total control over all circumstances.

Never before had I been able to sit still so long, content simply to be aware of God and worship Him. Never had God been so real before. A new understanding of tongues, transporting wings of the Spirit, was given me. My Teacher was teaching me to wait upon God.

Waiting upon God, had been a cliché before. I knew

just a little of what it meant, but essentially it was something with which I had had no firsthand experience.

Waiting upon God, I learned, is beholding Him. Looking to Him until He is seen for Who He really is. His Power, His Love, Mercy, Grace, Longsuffering, Goodness, Sovereignty, Wisdom. God is God, and it takes time to behold Him as the Holy Spirit glorifies Him to us.

Included in the phrase is the idea of submission. What is there to say to such a One? Can we advise Him? Can we stop Him on His course and tell Him He is wrong? Is there a place or a person where His power doesn't have sway? All we can do is submit. That may sound like fatalism, but the Christian is given absolute free will—the privilege of choosing to submit. If He can't see God, it is not easy. But once he can see who He is, how could he choose otherwise?

What a difference viewing life from the position of waiting on God made! No more fighting life and circumstances. No longer even seeing problems as problems, but rather new opportunities for God to reveal Himself as God. Every need, a receptacle for God's glory. From that position, all of life is cause to praise God.

I learned something else; waiting upon God is to expect of Him. This is probably the heart of the word. Not only seeing who He *is,* but expecting Him to *act, now,* in accordance with the revelation He has given us of Himself. Waiting is expecting God to be consistent with the picture of Him that the Bible has given us. And I saw that the opposite of expectancy was nothing less than unbelief.

The work of Jesus on the Cross became more real in the waiting. The glory, the triumph of it was made known, exactly as Jesus said, "When the Holy Ghost is come, He will glorify Me." He has taken sin away in the shedding of His Blood. He has taken us to death when He died. He has conquered Satan for us. Because of that work, we are more than conquerors. He is risen and ascended, and He has taken us to that heavenly dimension with Him. It is finished—not only for me, but for every person I meet. He is now Savior and Lord. Because of that finished work, every promise of God is made over to us. And because of that ascension, the Holy Spirit is given not only to me, but to all who will ask.

Now, looking at people and praying for them was a new and wondrous experience. Already their sin, bondage, had been dealt with. My proclamation, my praying, even my attitudes—all were transmuted in the light of that finished work.

Day after day, my Teacher had me wait before this glorious God, and what He had done. Prayer became almost exclusively praise. There was little else to do in the light of who He was, and what He had done.

Into my mind came the story of Jehoshaphat in II Chronicles 20, and it would come back to me many times. If ever a man was surrounded by impossible and insurmountable problems, let alone enemies, that was Jehoshaphat. His only response was to seek God, to wait upon Him.

The chapter records his prayer. It was all praise and worship. Its every line is filled with expectancy, almost vibrates with what He is going to do. His only request was a cry of helplessness that looked to God to do what He would. To this, God gave a word which said in effect: This problem is not your concern, but Mine—just trust Me.

They went out to face the problem, singing praise to

God, and as they did so, they discovered that God had already solved it. With delight, I knew I could go to face impossible situations with praise to God—singing hallelujahs.

During these days, the Spirit taught me when to sing praises and when to be silent. Both expressions of worship found their place.

I had never really sung His praises before, but now, at times, the vision of God was so glorious that saying praises, whether in English or tongues, was not enough. One day, for no reason, I began to *sing* the praise I would normally be saying. A gate was opened within my spirit, and the glory of God came in. From then on, singing praises became a regular part of my worship. I understood fully what Paul meant in I Corinthians 14—when he said that he would sing with the spirit also.

Other times the vision was equally glorious—but in a very different way. The awesomeness of God would fill the room. There was nothing to say. Any expression would have been an insult. All that could be expressed was said in dumb awe before Him. God was there. The whole world was hushed in His Presence.

These were different days when all restless activity was brought to experimental death, and a new activity was born that was directed not manward but Godward. A stillness, and a peace settled within. A song of praise began to ascend to God constantly. At times, I would wake up at night, praising God.

But when would action come? This was all so unorthodox! No testimony or book of successful pastoring had ever recommended doing *nothing*, but sit on the floor, wait, and worship God! I began to wonder if I was becoming some kind of fanatic. Yet, there was no doubt.

Turn Your Back on the Problem

I could never return to the old way. I couldn't go back, though I couldn't help wondering at times what lay ahead.

Then came an invitation to speak at the Elim Bible Institute, in upstate New York. I had heard both good and strange reports about the school. Both reports were extreme. It seemed that one either loved the place—or hated it. Most of the rumors I had heard were that they were sincere but awfully far-out. Yet some of my closest and most respected friends urged me to fellowship with them. I had shelved the matter months before, but now an invitation to lecture the students was on my desk. I accepted with curious anticipation, sensing strongly that I had to go.

The very first service I was in, the entire congregation began to do, as one man, what I had been doing alone in my study. Spontaneously they broke into song—hauntingly beautiful, unrecognizable, unlike anything I had ever heard before. Gently, soaring, uplifting, it was a tune taught by the Spirit, and a harmony brought about by the unseen Conductor. As my voice blended with theirs, not only did my heart thrill to the fellowship, but I felt immense joy in realizing that what He was teaching me, He had taught these people many years before.

If I was to be called odd, strange, fanatic—then so be it. The fellowship with God was worth any name anyone would put on me. I was committed more deeply than ever to the path of waiting upon God for what He should do.

The act of waiting upon God, means being woven together with Him—becoming one with Him. To exchange our strength for His strength.

The Holy Spirit had broken my trust in myself, and

now He was replacing it with a trust in Him and His ability. I didn't realize it at the time—but in all the aloneness with Him, I was exchanging strengths.

Slowly, gradually, thoroughly, I learned in every detail to choose to let Him take over and initiate action. Every moment was an opportunity for Him to live.

10

During these days of being shut up to worship and waiting upon God, another lesson that I had learned long ago in my head was made alive to me in my heart, to the point where an integral part of my ministry became a new experience.

When I was about sixteen years old, a green preacher, I searched for the way to minister life as well as the words of faith. I noticed that some preachers would preach excellent messages. They spoke truth, and when they sat down, I often had the urge to clap. But occasionally others would minister, who gave more. They, too, spoke truth—but it was delivered with the very Spirit of Truth Himself—and He ministered Life—Jesus was real and present in every word. When they were finished, I wanted to pray and glorify God. What was the difference? I didn't know, but I knew I wanted to join the latter class.

Turn Your Back on the Problem

In the church I was attending at the time, there was an old man, Brother Copsey, and I sensed he knew the answer. Every Sunday morning he would be in church, his bald head shining—a grin from ear to ear that was real joy bubbling through. When he got up to pray or praise the Lord, it was obvious he knew God on a very personal basis. His big rough laborer's hands would grasp mine, and he would call down the blessing of God upon me. Although a layman, he went far and wide on his old black bicycle, preaching and praying for the sick. He had unusual results. He may not have been a professional, but he had power, and people found Jesus when he was there.

One day I visited with him, and posed my question, "What is the secret of preaching?" I asked simply. He peered long at me over his glasses as if debating whether he should impart such highly classified information.

"Got any books?" His deep voice rumbled, as his eyes pinned me to my chair. He assumed I had, and went directly to his point: "Burn 'em!" He paused to let the shock register. It did. "If you want to hear God and get a message from Him—you get alone—and I mean real alone. Go to the woods and sit on a log. Wait with your whole soul on Him. Wait until you hear the birds sing and the leaves rustle--" He leaned forward in his chair, his voice lowering, "then listen to Him. He'll talk to you deep inside. When you are quiet enough, you'll hear. Then worship Him."

I saw it, and such was the power of the moment that I could but nod dumbly, which I did, a little like a wooden puppet.

He continued, with a whispered intensity that was

almost palpable. "Then take your Bible, but, before you open it, ask Him to talk to you. Be still, as you read it, and listen for Him. Read it again and listen for Him. He'll tell you more than all them educated professors and their foolish books." I ignored the sudden thought of my love of libraries; our hearts were as one, and the Holy Spirit was pouring revelation into my spirit. I was learning more in seconds than I had in months.

"And when He's done talking, you'll have a message that won't keep in—and the people will get it when you talk, and it will work in 'em."

From that day on, I began to strive for stillness before God. I would try to listen carefully for Him, whenever I prepared a message. I would try to meditate on the Scriptures. That conversation was some sixteen years previous, but it had had a more profound effect on all my ministry than anything I had learned since.

Now the Holy Spirit had shut me up to worship and wait on God, and all that I had spasmodically tried to do for years began to happen. He was the Teacher now, and He was working in me to will and to do His good pleasure. It was like learning to meditate all over again—except that this time I wasn't trying to achieve anything. He was accomplishing it in me. I found myself being bonded to words, sentences, for days at a time, while He explained them to me. I didn't burn my books, anymore than I had at the beginning, but I found that the Holy Spirit forbade me to read books or commentaries until He had first made a given verse come alive to me with *His* meaning. Then, and only then, did I have liberty to see what other men thought.

Meditation is so much more than reading the Bible, I

discovered. It involves reading and re-reading until one sees what is *really* being said—the whole picture of what the Holy Spirit, who is the Author of the Word, intended for us to see. It may mean re-reading until memorization takes place, but one must stay with it until the Teacher closes that particular lesson. Nor is just seeing it from every angle enough. That's just the half of it. Then it has to be assimilated, worked into the clay of our very lives.

A verse from the Bible is taken, even a paragraph or whole chapter, and it is rolled around in our heart, viewed from every conceivable angle, as the Holy Spirit directs one's thoughts. The original Hebrew meaning of the word indicates that it is turned over within, until one ends up muttering to oneself about it.

This is the actual chewing and digestion of God's Word. We chew our food, swallow it, and after it is digested, it becomes our cells and muscles. Even so, to digest God's Word in meditation is to become mature—to build spiritual muscles.

But the meditation doesn't stop even there. It must then be brought into an active role in the routine of our living and doing. It is thus that God's Word brings life—life in our lives, and life in the lives of others through our lives.

The Holy Spirit took me to Peter's first epistle and began to make it alive. So alive, that I was gripped by the first words for days at a time. Even when I would leave the study, sit at the table, drink coffee in a restaurant, or drive my car to and from the church, the words kept returning. "Blessed be the God and Father of our Lord Jesus Christ who according to His great mercy had caused us to be born again to a living hope through the resurrection of Jesus Christ from the dead . . ." They would go around and around within, and with each new round, a fresh view of truth would be given; new light would pour on the familiar words.

There were times when I would be overwhelmed by a sudden rush of truth that would come from the words. Every place became in reality holy ground. Wherever we went, the Teacher and I, He would simply declare school in session, and that was that. He was there in the restaurants, and riding in the car, teaching me the mind and thoughts of God.

The revelations of truth were not new doctrine. It was old, familiar doctrine, suddenly coming alive and catching fire. And something interesting began to happen. I began to be conscious that my attitudes and desires were being changed. Not only was He speaking through the Word, and building it into me by meditation, but the lordship of Jesus over my life was becoming a reality. He was commanding me quietly and surely from within. He was encouraging me when I needed it. This was God's living Word.

I had always believed God—even believed Him rather recklessly at times—but now all the old promises came alive, and He led me through them, word by word, turning them over within, and challenging me with what He planned to do. He made me *know* a promise in meditation. No longer words—a direct assurance from Him to me. And with that, suddenly faith was a natural. Faith had come by hearing God's word spoken within.

Jeremiah said, "Thy words were found and I did eat

101

them, and they were the joy and rejoicing of my heart." Such joy was mine. Many times praise and thanksgiving would rise within for hours at the revelation of His word.

Something else began to happen: everything around me, all the people and problems that came into my life, even the things I merely heard about, began to be a running commentary on what He had given me to meditate on. It was as if the Teacher, having showed me truth, would then arrange things to underscore the lesson. I still don't understand that and doubt that I ever will, but I could hear Him saying, "See what I mean?" or "This is how it works." It got to the point where, after meditating for a while, I took it for granted that very soon after, there would be a living demonstration of the truth or principle, or I would meet a situation that demanded action on the basis of the meditating, or I would need the special wisdom that I had just been given. My whole life had become a teaching experience—every waking moment—with the Holy Sprit as the Instructor.

One day He spoke to me from I Peter 2. *Be yourselves built* ... The words grabbed hold of me, and I waited for the answer to what He was saying. Then I saw it so clearly, I danced for joy. A brick could not build itself into a building. All it could do was allow a master builder to build it. I was a living stone, and He, the master builder. He was teaching me to live in the passive voice. To *be built,* and not build myself. All of these promises and statements of truth I read were not calling me to try and make them come to pass, but simply to accept the promise as mine—thank Him for it, and then let Him raise me to live on the plane He had shown me.

Turn Your Back on the Problem

The Bible became a new book of revelation, as the Holy Spirit made it alive—revealing Jesus on every page, and then Himself lifting me to live within its light.

Worship became a deeper and richer experience, for not only did the meditated word give direction and challenge, and become the stepping-stones to faith, but it also opened windows to God. Every line seemed to say, "God is like this!" and my heart melted before it. *"God is really like this!"* My heart could hardly believe it. How much of my ministry had been words, phrases and doctrine. Seeds sown over the years. Seeds of truth were now springing into life and growing under His touch.

There were days when the Scripture seemed unyielding. Days when I would just stare at the verses, and they would stare back. But instead of getting frustrated or impatient, I had by now learned something, and I just waited upon God. And I came to find that those days preceded Glory! For God was ploughing deep within, and producing a capacity for Him that I did not have before. When those days came, heaven would seem a million miles away, yet still the Spirit bade me wait. When *He* felt it was right, He gave me an awareness of God again.

Each day led me further and further away from the horrible emptiness of pre-November. A new life, a new ministry was being formed and shaped. And it was being done in His time, not mine.

Out of the hours He shut me up to wait on Him and meditate on His Word, something else began to grow. I became aware of His Presence at all times, even in the frantic pace of New York City. I had read books on the practice of God's continual presence, and had not been able to achieve it, no matter how hard I strived. Now, I suddenly realized it was growing, of its own accord.

The first time I realized it, I was hanging from a subway strap at a quarter past five on one of the hottest days I could remember. It seemed that all of Brooklyn had to get into the one subway car; we were so packed in that we were literally holding each other up. There was an odor of sweat and garlic. The fan was broken so there was nothing to move the air that we shared, which actually tasted acrid on the lips. The brakes shrieked, jangling every nerve, as the train lurched to a stop at Times Square. I held my breath waiting for the pressure to ease. But no one got out. Not one. Instead, half of Manhattan seemed determined to get *in.* And somehow they did. Sweat was now rolling down my face, stinging my eyes . . . and I could not reach my hand up to wipe it away.

The train pulled away into the subterranean darkness. The wheels roared and squealed. It was then that I became aware that I was, and had been, praising God—deep, very deep within. I was aware that a great peace possessed me—a joy was dancing inside, and throughout my being was praise to God. The wonder was that I had become *aware* that I was praising God. I was still and quiet within, worshiping Him without even thinking or trying or telling myself I ought to.

I noticed something else; without my consciously praying for them, those people touching me that I could see seemed to be taking on some of my peace. It struck me than that we live on two levels at once. When the spirit is trained to look only to God, listen only for Him, even to be worshiping Him we do so almost unconsciously. The body may be swinging precariously from a subway strap, our mind may be thinking a problem through, but at the same time, we can be alone with God in worship in our spirit. Now I could understand, "Pray without ceasing;" and "I will bless the Lord at all times His praise shall continually be in my mouth." All circumstances are holy, nothing is secular, for we are priests to Him in vital communion with Him.

When I got back to my office that day, I thanked Him for the multitude of lessons that He was teaching me. And then I couldn't help asking what He already knew was on my heart: what about some action in church-building? I knew a great change had taken place in *me*—so great that every part of me was transformed—but I doubted that anyone else had seen or felt a difference. The church was still basically the same, and souls were still not getting saved. Nothing had really happened, I knew it had to happen soon.

"Well?"

Have you so soon forgotten the first lesson I taught you? Do you want to be in charge again?

"No! Please!"

Then be still and know that I am God.

11

I had no idea how He would build His church, but I *knew* that He would. I did not know what part I was to play, and it was not for me to know, so I simply waited and worshiped. I did come to realize that His work at that time was exclusively in *me.*

The first hint of what might be coming was almost unnoticed. The phone rang one morning. It was Trudy Johnson. Trudy was a radiant young housewife, living in Flatbush—on the east side of Brooklyn. She was no public speaker or talker, but she wanted so badly to share Jesus with everyone she knew.

A couple of years before, I had conducted meetings in a home forty-five miles north of the city. A number of people had found Christ, deeply and intimately, and a branch work had opened there, where Tom Hatcher was now pastor. Trudy had experienced those services, and believed that what she had seen in the suburbs, could happen in the city. I had come back with similar feelings and had tried to make small home meetings happen. But it had failed miserably and joined the junk-pile of busted ideas.

This time, when Trudy called, it was different—I was different. God's dealings in me had taken all the trying out of me. Trudy had continued to ask for home meetings in her area—and having been burned badly once, I had put her off. But now I felt a distinct witness of the Spirit: this was it. I was about to see the mighty hand of God.

That first Tuesday night, I actually trembled as I drove through the unfamiliar streets of Flatbush. What was God going to do? Something, that's all I knew. And He didn't like me reaching up to get a glimpse of His blueprint. When I walked through the door, at 8:00 P.M., the place was not exactly crowded.

Trudy, a friend and her daughter, and later, we were joined by three others. All were curious, and more than a little nervous—as was I.

Briefly, I shared the Person of Jesus, what He had done in His death and resurrection, and gave my own testimony of how I came to know Christ. Slowly, hesitantly, the little group shared with each other what they knew or didn't know of Christ. Then we had some coffee and cake and departed.

Driving home that night, I could hardly consider that the meeting had been a staggering success. Yet I knew, as undramatic or spectacular as this was, that the Holy Spirit had been there. And I was not dismayed. In fact, there had been a throb of life about it that was thrilling: I knew that God had begun to build His church.

Turn Your Back on the Problem

We had arranged to return in two weeks. This time, after the six of us got there, the doorbell continued to ring. Before long, sixteen people were gathered in the room. As we waited for the latecomers to arrive, everyone happily chatted with a sense of anticipation. I looked around the group—every kind of person was there. A Jew sat over in the corner, a number of Roman Catholics—housewives and businessmen. Finally, a quiet came, almost as if someone offstage had signaled for silence.

As I stood up, I prayed that Jesus would be seen and not Malcolm Smith. And again, I simply presented Him and who He was—the Son of God. He had died for us—He was risen and had a claim upon our lives. And I invited discussion. One or two testified how they had met Jesus Christ; others asked sincere questions. Gradually, I gathered that these people were sick and tired of the established church. In quiet desperation, they were seeking for a *real* God and a *real* faith.

It seemed that we had hardly begun before it was 10:30. We broke for coffee, but no one left, 'and I was still talking of Jesus Christ, and the meaning of commitment to Him, at midnight.

Pulling my car into the garage that night, or rather, early morning, I had to remind myself to stop singing because people were trying to sleep. But the tune would not leave my mind: "God is moving by His Spirit . . ."

Two more weeks went by, and now people were jamming into the home where we held the meetings. Discussion moved quickly and easily. Fresh testimonies flowed from those who were just now coming to know Jesus.

At one meeting, a young housewife sat on the edge of

her chair drinking in every word, throwing the hardest questions she knew how. Her name was Dottie Kane, and she smoked constantly and wore a half-cynical look, as she was told of a living Jesus who was able to come into a life, and bring about rebirth. Dottie had sought God in Protestant and Catholic circles, and was now a humanist, a do-good-to-my-neighbor. Totally immersed in all the social action she could put her hand to, she had been to a meeting on drug abuse. At that meeting, she met Lorraine, who took Dotty and her husband Richard home for coffee. Lorraine had accepted Christ at a Billy Graham Crusade years earlier, and had been to our first two meetings. She spoke of Jesus Christ as she would a personal friend. It shook Dotty, in her crumbled faith, and she accepted Lorraine's invitation to study the Bible in the home.

She now sat hardly believing what she heard. Shaking her head and pitying us, she went home, took out the large family Bible, and began reading—searching for the proof she wanted. It couldn't be true; we had to be fanatics. But late that night, in the Book of Acts, she found instead, reference to the kind of dynamic Christianity which she had seen and heard.

The next meeting she returned, this time with the family Bible under her arm, to check us out on the spot. By this time, others were committing their entire lives to Christ, as a result of the meeting. The atmosphere was positively electric, as testimonies flowed from those who were now living proof of what was being said.

Dotty, her big Bible open on her knees, was beginning to see that the Scripture knew of no other Christianity. This *was* Christianity! It wasn't religion, buildings, organizations, ceremony, ritual—it was receiving Jesus Christ as Lord of all, and receiving forgiveness, a righteousness from God through the Blood of Jesus shed two thousand years ago. It was all beginning to make unbelievable sense.

The next week, Richard was with her. He had played in jazz bands, knew the world and all its ways. And he was an insurance broker, with little or no time for relevant God. How could God be relevant in a world of dog eat dog? He sat and listened, feeling nervous and out of place as people freely shared beliefs and experiences deeper than he had ever heard expressed aloud.

God continued to work His purpose out—not always as quickly as we might have liked, but in the long run, far more quickly than we would have dared hope for. Five more meetings passed, and both Richard and Dotty gave their lives unconditionally to Christ. They did it alone at home, the same week—*each not knowing that the other had done it.* When they finally told each other, to their joy, they found that they were both disciples of Jesus.

It wasn't long before they had been baptized in the Holy Spirit. Richard handed his insurance business over to God, and life became a daily adventure with Jesus in control.

From this core, the seeds for other home meetings grew, and soon both Floyd and I were involved almost every night we could spare. In each case, the pattern followed that original meeting in Flatbush.

Days were flying by, filled with meetings in homes, meetings with inquiring individuals in restaurants, or in the office. Telephone calls, committee meetings, preaching engagements—I looked back with not a little longing to that season during which He had separated me unto Himself to prepare me—and to think I had wondered when He would ever get on with it! Pressing church business, visiting the sick and shut-ins—I was caught in a whirlpool that was spinning faster and faster, and I would soon be choked with activity. Activity that was a result of stillness!

One day in May, I went to my office and locked the door. I had been shown a key by the Holy Spirit, but I was in danger of losing the key in activity. Floyd shared the work, but I was still carrying the burden of not only the meetings, but also the administration, and a hundred other things that had to be done.

I felt a nudge in my heart to get rid of some of that burden in order to be able to wait upon God. Acts 6 came into my head, and I knew that that was where the answer would be. I pulled out my dog-eared New Testament and knelt beside my desk.

It seemed that the early church had an administration problem, too, and had asked the apostles to come and work out the details. Their response was that it did not make sense for them to leave prayer and God's word to serve as administrators. They did not dismiss the problem, however, but recognized that administration was a real ministry that would make the church function correctly. They found men who obviously enjoyed administration and who were eminently qualified, spiritual, and they turned the task over to them.

I flipped over the pages to the Epistles, where the Bible spoke of the ministry of administrators.

I felt almost guilty thinking of finding such a ministry. Many men of God I knew had no such luxury. Why should I count myself privileged? At almost every ministers' get-together I'd been to, we shared how we didn't have time for the really necessary things.

Getting up from the floor, I paced the room. My eyes turned to an advertisement on the desk—on its way to the wastebasket. Almost without thinking, I picked it up to read it.

It was a chatty letter to ministers. It began by telling us how busy we were with committees, visiting, civic functions and church business. In the light of that, it was obvious, it continued, that you do not have time to do things like prepare sermons and get original messages from God—so they would do it for us. A happy little paragraph told how we could send a fee and receive our messages pre-prepared and pre-outlined each week, and that hundreds of men of God of all denominations were already availing themselves of this time-saving service. I crumpled the letter and threw it in the wastebasket. "So that's the alternative, is it? Well, I don't care if I am the only minister in the country who recognizes the ministry of administration, I am going to."

Falling to my knees again, I praised God for what He had showed me about worship and waiting. I gave myself anew to Him, to be His in the unique ministry He had given me, and I trusted Him to give us an administrator.

Almost at once, Floyd came to my mind. After further prayer, I was sure that he was the man; but it would have to witness to his spirit every bit as clearly as it did to mine. We lunched together that day, and I shared my thoughts with him. And it did witness to him as being truly of the Lord.

I turned the church over to him, as far as its

administration was concerned, every detail of running it. I was free to wait on God, to counsel those with spiritual problems, and to give myself to evangelism in the homes, and teaching in the church.

What followed was a unique and profound learning experience as we learned to exercise our respective ministries. It took time for the church to get used to the idea, but as weeks turned into months, it was overwhelmingly proven and approved of.

The days settled down to a schedule of waiting on God for as many hours as could be given, for Him to continue to deal with *me*. Other times were given to studying for the weekend teaching services. The rest of the day and night was given to counseling and evangelism.

I had never been so hilariously happy. Every week brought some new development in someone's life. Someone one night would be filled with the Spirit, a miracle of healing would take place the next day, and more souls would surrender to Jesus the following night. And throughout, there was the unparalleled joy of teaching new converts how to walk with God.

God was building His church the way He wanted it. Because I had gotten out of the way, and because I was gladly letting Him get on with the major reconstruction job He wanted to do inside of me. It seemed at times that there was so much renovation going on inside of me that there wasn't any more that could be done—and then another wall would be knocked through.

I thought He had done a lot—but it was only the beginning.

12

A good deal of my schedule was employed in traveling on speaking engagements. During flights, I used to talk to the person sitting next to me with my primary concern that I had to do a work for God. By any means, this person *had* to be spoken to about Jesus Christ, even if the conversation were twisted and forced to the subject.

It now became obvious to me that it was not my job to initiate a conversation, but rather to leave that to the Holy Spirit. I was free to love the person sitting in front of me; I was not uptight trying to manipulate them to Christ. While I loved them, the Holy Spirit was doing His work. I was now free to truly listen to the man. I had no idea where the conversation was heading. It was mine to give myself wholly to this person, listen to him, and listen to Him for what He had to say.

The idea that there always needed to be a firm explanation of the Gospel was also dismissed. The Holy

Spirit used the entire Body of Christ in bringing about the regeneration of an individual. It might be for me to bring a man to conviction of needs, for another to bring him to repentance, and faith in Christ, but all of us rested in the Commander, who was working all things together in His Infinite Wisdom.

This had all become very real to me, as I waited before the Lord. When the summer came, and the camp-meeting season started, it became increasingly evident. Witnessing to the unconverted and sharing with the family of God was no longer a hit-or-miss affair. It was under His direction, but *beautifully natural and spontaneous.*

Each day, He brought individuals into my life. At one time I often looked upon them as intrusions or interruptions. Now I saw them as part of His Plan, even if they upset my pre-conceived plans. Before, I would have searched my brain for the way to answer or share with them. Now, I was free to love them, listen fully, asking and receiving His Wisdom to answer.

It was a glorious experience—sometimes sowing, sometimes reaping, but always conscious of being in complete harmony with *the* Evangelist and *the* Revivalist: the Holy Spirit.

After a camp meeting in Western Canada in July, I had to change planes in Toronto. I waited in the departure lounge, and looked over the people waiting with me for the Air Canada flight to Kennedy Airport. It was vacation time, and there were the usual vacationers flying for the first time—the pitch of their conversation betraying their nervousness. Tired, bored business-

116

men—with their briefcases between their knees, reading the *Wall Street Journal*. A few carried bags prominently displaying Pan Am labels for Europe. I smiled—all packaged for a fly-from-reality-pay-later plan. They were obviously picking up a flight in Kennedy. A few hippies who insisted on sitting on the floor, completed our flight.

The flight was announced in French and English, and we moved wearily toward the walkway to the jet. My mind was very full, as I had a few days at home before flying to Liberia, to speak to native pastors and missionaries. Jean and the children were going directly to England, where we were to meet.

The Lord had spoken very definitely to me that I was to go to West Africa, and had also given me a series of messages that I was to speak. A week after He had spoken, I had received the invitation to go to Liberia to speak at the Workers Conference of the Liberian Christian Assemblies. It was now only days away—and the messages given so directly by the Holy Spirit occupied almost all my thoughts.

I sank into my seat and fastened my safety belt. My spirit reached out to the Lord, thanking Him for the wonderful camp meetings I had just returned from—and for all He had been doing since I was in Salem. Then I turned my attention to my fellow passengers.

"Thank You, Father, that You are Love. That all these people are Your concern. You love them. Thank You, that You are the Living God, and You are now working in their lives, whether they know it or not. Some of them are hearing Your voice: some of them do not recognize it yet. All Wise Father, You know exactly what each of these people need.

"I am Yours to do with what You will. If You want me

117

to speak to anyone on this plane—here I am—You arrange the opportunity, and You give me the words . . ."

I relaxed and got out my note pad, to see if there were any further messages He might have for Africa.

Coffee was served, and almost before we had settled down, we began to descend into our landing pattern. No one had been spoken to, no witness made. Thank You, Lord.

"This is your captain speaking. We have just been advised that we shall not be able to land at Kennedy Airport for another forty-five minutes, due to traffic congestion. Please bear with us in this inconvenience."

A groan arose from the passengers, and I thanked the Lord for whatever reason we were to stay aloft. I felt sorry for Jean and the children down on the ground somewhere, hoped that they were praising God for His purpose, too, and continued to meditate and work.

The plane droned on and on, around and around. People became restless and frustration permeated the cabin atmosphere. Then the captain spoke again, "We have been advised of a further delay of one hour before we can land. We shall be returning to Toronto for refueling."

The words hit the cabin of the jet like an announcement of a Wall Street crash.

Everyone began talking at once, taking out their helpless anger on anyone within hearing distance. Others began to loudly share their plans for the revamping of New York City.

Sitting across the aisle was a woman in her thirties—one of those with a Pan Am label on her flight bag. She looked at me in horror, almost anger, and began to speak to me in a tone that suggested that I had somehow caused the delay.

"But that means I'm going to miss my connection in New York. I'm on my way to Europe tonight—this can't be happening." My interest was aroused. "Which part? I'm from Europe."

"Oh! I'm going all over—visiting all the sights and cities. I'm off to forget my problems, drown my sorrows and come back full of life." She laughed, but there was a brittle edge to it.

It had been a long time since I had heard anyone so openly admitting to escape from reality.

Suddenly she looked so pathetic sitting there, all ticketed and mapped out and labeled for Europe—a trip that I knew would be another dead-end for her.

A compassion that came from Him welled up in me, and I felt His nudge. I launched out directly. "You'll never find an answer to your trouble in Europe, or anywhere on this planet. You certainly won't come back with life. Just more disillusionment!" I had said it as gently as I possibly could, but the words hit like hammer-blows on the glass facade.

"Why, what an awful thing to say to a perfect stranger," she said, trying to make light of it, and failing so miserably that we both knew it hadn't worked. "Tell me, do you always go around brightening people's lives that way?" I shook my head and said nothing. "Then what do you mean?" She tried to make the words sound casual and was visibly dismayed by their obvious urgency.

"I mean that the answer to our sorrows, our emptiness—in fact, the answer to life itself, is not an 'it'—an environment, or a philosophy, or a geographical location—the "it" is a Person, Jesus Christ."

She smiled and scrambled back to familiar ground. "I go to church, and I'm involved in a lot of community work ..." she warmed to her subject, and I listened with love and without interrupting, as she detailed her various activities on behalf of her fellowman. Then, she became very serious, hesitating for a moment, looking at me as if searching to see if she could really trust me. "My husband died a year ago, just when we were beginning to live and to really enjoy each other. Since then, life has lost all meaning. It's been pretty much downhill all the way. I have pills to make me sleep—and pills to get me up. I'm in analysis, but honestly, I wind up comforting my psychiatrist. Unless I get away and forget everything, I don't know--" and her voice broke.

"Can I tell you about some people I know—one in particular?" She nodded, so I continued.

"I knew a young housewife, named Ruth. It wasn't a tragedy that came into her life, but she just sort of—snapped. Her life was lived inside a shell of depression and fear. The whole world seemed to be covered with a black cloud. Today, she is radiant, always spilling her joy over to others. In fact, friends and even strangers meet in her home every week to catch some of it. Her husband, Peter, caught the same joy, even though he had no great problem, outside of his wife's mental depression, and they are more alive now than they have ever been at any time in their lives."

"All right, I'll bite: what happened? Where did she go? What treatment did she receive?" The woman leaned across the aisle, and I couldn't help noticing that the people behind her were listening behind *Time* and *Life* magazines. I would liked it to have been more private, but there was no turning back now.

"As I said before, the answer is not in a thing or location, but in Jesus Christ. He is alive. He walked into Ruth's life, and that was the beginning of the miracle that He is continuing to work every day in and through her."

A puzzled look came on her face. "I go to church, but I'm afraid the whole thing rather bores me. I just sit and think of my problems until it's all over." She lit a cigarette and blew smoke into the air. "Who are you anyway?"

"Me? Well, I work full-time introducing people to Jesus Christ. I do it in homes, planes, anywhere I am. I also do it regularly from a pulpit, in a church."

"The way you talk about Him," she said wistfully, "it's almost as if He were real." She looked away, out the window at the piles of clouds, red-gold in the setting sun. "There are some neighbors of mine who talk that way. They have meetings in their home, to study the Bible."

I leaned forward. "Do you know, we do that almost every night of the week? Do they attend a church?"

"Oh, it's a strange place . . . What do they call it . . . Pente—something like that."

"Have you ever been there?"

"No, but I've been tempted to. What do they mean by receiving Jesus? They are always so happy, talking about it."

I was in awe at the efficiency of the Holy Spirit. He had been working in this woman's life, echoing in her empty heart, but she hadn't quite recognized it. He had used her neighbors and now one of His servants, on a plane that was heading back to Toronto! Only He could work like this.

I began to explain how much God loved her, enough to send His only Son Jesus to bear our sins and sorrow in His body on the Cross, shedding His Blood to cleanse our sin, bringing us into His Presence. She hung on every word.

"I would like that—how could I do it?" I opened my Bible, and read from Romans 10:8-11, 13 (TLB).

> For salvation that comes from trusting Christ—which is what we preach—is already within easy reach of each of us; in fact, it is as near as our own hearts and mouths. For if you tell others with your own mouth that Jesus Christ is your Lord, and believe in your own heart that God has raised him from the dead, you will be saved.
> For it is by believing in his heart that a man becomes right with God; and with his mouth he tells others of his faith, confirming his salvation. For the Scriptures tell us that no one who believes in Christ will ever be disappointed. Anyone who calls upon the name of the Lord will be saved.

She looked straight in my eyes and nodded ever so slightly. "You know, I think I'm going to do that."

The stewardess' voice interrrupted; "Make sure your seat belts are fastened, please, and your seats are in an upright position. We are on final approach for Toronto International Airport."

Turn Your Back on the Problem

We landed smoothly and taxied to the terminal building. All passengers for the European flight were immediately transferred. I never saw that woman again, but I know she had found the One who arranged that return trip to Toronto.

We waited for forty-five minutes in Toronto, and I spent the whole time quietly worshiping God for His Great Wisdom. Later, leaning back in my seat as we took off again, I praised Him. "Thank You, Lord. You are the best air traffic controller Kennedy Airport ever had!"

13

One day as I was meditating in my office, it came to me that I hadn't even noticed what was happening to our church. We had done no advertising of the special meetings, yet the people came. There was no personality behind the meetings; no one knew who would be conducting which. It was obvious what was happening: the Holy Spirit Himself, the Director, the Invisible Commander of the Church of Jesus Christ, was quietly, powerfully building. He was not using one person, but everyone in this wonderful adventure.

The miracle that was happening in the homes had spread to the church. We did not advertise our church to the home groups, nor did we make a point of inviting folks to come, but they came anyway, to see what it was like in a church where all the membership were committed Christians.

Turn Your Back on the Problem

New faces from different nationalities began to fill the pews on Sunday mornings. The home meetings became outposts that fed into the church services. New converts and seeking people found their way to Fourth Avenue and 54th Street.

More amazing still, something was happening to the thinking regarding Fourth Avenue and 54th Street. It was beginning to be understood that the building on the corner was not the church. The church met inside it. The church was the people—people who had committed their lives to Jesus Christ, the Living, unconditionally His to do with as He pleased. They were the living stones, built upon Christ, the Living Foundation. Wherever they went, there was the church. On weekends, we gathered and were taught, and worshiped God together. During the week, we were scattered and were in the world, lights shining in the darkness, salt rubbed into the corruption of the world.

It forcibly hit us that we were all priests unto God, that we all had a ministry to God, and to others.

It wasn't just a matter of going to church on Sunday. How could you "go" to church anyway, when you were one of the living stones that made it? The church of born-again people could meet. That living church would then exercise their priestly ministry and worship God freely together, by the leading of the Spirit. A new sense of worship swept through the church, a spirit that had been there many years before, and now was coming back. The wind who blows where He will, was stirring us again. Gradually, a spirit of spontaneous worship became stronger, until it culminated at the Annual Convention's Saturday service. After the ministry of the Word of God, the congregation began to praise God, then began to sing praise. This had never happened before. The large convention gathering sang a melody spontaneously, given them by the Holy Spirit. Each one seemed to have his own part and sang in glorious harmony. The words were praise to God, and all stood and worshiped God. I stood on the platform, part of the whole. But I was not in charge; someone else was in control here.

Suddenly, there was silence. A living silence. Everyone had become still at once. Someone spoke out in tongues, and this was followed at once by the Gift of Interpretation, a strong, clear message of encouragement. The congregation moved on into worshiping song.

This has not happened since, nor would anyone try to make it happen. Ours is the Holy Spirit's church, and He does as He pleases.

Communion services became longer as the congregation just sat and ministered to the Lord, testifying of His greatness. During one such service, as Jesus was exalted in praise, five people were instantly healed as they sat in their seats. We certainly believe in healing, and the sick are prayed for regularly, but this was the power of the Holy Spirit moving spontaneously among us.

The constant trickle of newly saved people, thrilled with Jesus, coming in from the home Bible studies, lent a quiet enthusiasm to everything.

All this time, we were beholders. It was made abundantly clear to us that this was God's work, not ours. We never knew what a meeting would be like. Some were noisy, almost hilarious with joy. Others were quiet, seemingly uneventful. A few were perfectly still, under the awful hush of God's Presence. And still the people came and found Jesus.

One lady slipped into the church and had scarcely sat

down, when she began to sob, overwhelmed by God's Presence. This happened every time she came. Finally, she yielded to Him, accepting Jesus as Lord of her life, and very shortly she was baptized in the Holy Spirit. All her life she had gone to a certain church, but it was only now that she actually felt God, and knew that He was alive and loved her.

If the church of living stones, scattered throughout the week, witnessing and proclaiming Jesus into the darkness, coming together to worhip on Friday nights and Sundays, was to mature, they needed teaching. The Sunday services became less and less evangelistic, and more and more teaching, introducing old and new converts to the rich truths in the Word of God. And in all there was a growing sense that the work had only begun.

In the late summer, invitations to minister and teach at other churches were pouring in. One morning, five letters lay on my desk, asking for teaching crusades. Floyd's wife, Judy, who was my secretary, laughed and said, "Do you think God is trying to tell you something?"

I wondered. Was He? Was it time to leave now, and launch into another kind of ministry? I could leave now without running away. I wondered. I had learned what He could do, when I got out of the way.

I knew I had to settle the question, and so, taking Floyd and an associate, we went to a country home and waited on God in prayer and fasting for three days.

Kneeling in the bedroom hour after hour, wrapped around with a sleeping bag against the chill of early fall,

Turn Your Back on the Problem

I thrilled at the difference between this time and the previous December. No fear or frustration—just listening for orders.

Then He spoke. Clearly and unmistakably. He told me to return to Brooklyn, and to be His intercessor among the people of that place. The joy at His orders was quite supernatural. For He shared with me what He was going to do in the future.

That night, I returned to Brooklyn and told the board something of what had transpired. As a board, we decided to call the church to prayer and waiting upon God in the light of what He had said. As we made the decision, the Holy Spirit fell upon us, and the board sang, praised, clapped, and came near to dancing in the Spirit for two hours. I knew that we had only begun to see what God had in mind.

All that was happening—I had once tried to make happen. Now, with my back to the problem, and my eyes on the Great God, waiting only on Him—it was happening beyond our wildest dreams.

It was New Year's Eve, 1971!

The church had been downstairs in the basement for a fellowship meal, and now we were gathered in the main auditorium. In a few moments we would have a time of sharing and holy communion as we began the New Year.

I looked over the gathering congregation. So many of these people could not have been here a year ago. Halfway back, on the left side, was a former cynic who a year earlier would have laughed out loud at the thought of being in church on New Year's Eve. In the front row was a housewife, who a year before had been trying to find meaning in life by smoking marijuana. Now she had found meaning in Christ. The place was filled with former seekers, young and old, who had looked in every garbage can in the alley—occult, oriental, affluent, humanist, political, philosophical—until Someone had finally directed their gaze upward. Some stood in groups, while others sat and prayed quietly. Expectancy was in the air.

The Holy Spirit had done this. Every person who had come to Christ in the past year had been a direct result of a work of the Holy Spirit. We had used no gimmicks, no drives, no special speakers. We had been obedient and done as He told us, and this was the result. Even if I had wanted to, I could not take the credit for any of these people being here. Every member of the congregation had been involved, and we were all recognizing in growing humility that we had been united under the direction of the Holy Spirit.

He was still directing. Strangers were scattered throughout the gathering congregation. They had sat at our round tables downstairs and had heard Christians share Jesus. Now, they were open to the Jesus they had seen alive in people.

Suddenly, a group of blue-jeaned, shaggy-haired teenagers sauntered in at the back. There was nothing new in this: we were rapidly becoming an international church, with every strata of society represented.

I couldn't help smiling as the fellows and girls were warmly greeted by everyone standing at the back. The service began. We sang with holy enthusiasm, the testimonies started, it was impossible to get a word in. One after another rose to his feet. Here a miraculous salvation; over in another corner a healing, from the middle of the crowd, someone shares a verse of Scripture that has come alive. Most of the people testifying were new converts. I smiled as some of the older members tried to come in with a testimony and were swamped by the new converts!

Turn Your Back on the Problem

I thanked God for those members of long standing, many of whom had prayed for years for this very thing to happen, and now they praised God with us for what we saw. It was their faithfulness that had kept the doors open. They had stood by me, particularly when I did not merit it. I thanked God for them all. The time flew by, and finally Floyd had to draw the testimonies to a close. I shared something from the Word of God, and we came to worship and communion.

Someone began to sing, "O, come let us adore Him—Christ the Lord." My mind went back vividly to those days in the Virgin Islands. I could hear again the hot-dog stand radio blasting that same song out over the sand. What had God wrought in that year—one year! The change in me was like night and day. Before me, was the evidence that He had done, and was doing, no more than He said He would.

The congregation was sitting praising Jesus. Their hands were raised, and they softly adored Him who had died for them, and was now alive.

He was really *there*. His Presence filled the building. Underneath us a subway train rumbled. A police siren wailed by—its red light reflecting on the windows of the church. But we were in another world. The heavenly places, giving glory to God through Jesus Christ.

"This is my body, which is broken for you." I broke the bread, and passed it to the deacons, who in turn shared it with the congregation.

"He was wounded for my transgressions—

He was bruised for our iniquities,

The chastisement that would bring us peace, was upon Him--

By His stripes we are healed."

I repeated the words from Isaiah slowly, letting their full meaning be written on their hearts by the Spirit. It was because of this that I had met with God in the Virgin Islands. If there was one thing that I had come to know as never before, it was this: my sin, my failure, my total unworthiness, was laid upon Christ. His Blood cleansed me to the depths and made me whole. I had known it since I was a teenager, but the Holy Spirit had made me to know it so very deeply in the past eighteen months. The words of my letter of resignation came back to me, "I myself am in need of a spiritual revival that I cannot find." By grace greater than any definition I could find, I had found that personal revival through a new appreciation of the Blood of Jesus, through a new revelation of Jesus Himself, and through the blinding revelation of the Holy Spirit that gave me true sight.

I quoted more from that chapter, feeling its depths within my own soul. "All we like sheep have gone astray. We have turned everyone to his own way, and the Lord had laid upon Him the iniquity of us all." We joined as one body in praise to Him. We were a group of sinners, forgiven and cleansed through Christ—now one body praising Him.

As the deacons returned to the front of the church, someone began to sing—"At the Cross, at the Cross, where I first saw the light . . ." It seemed to express our deepest feelings, as it rose to the Holy of Holies.

I looked over the people. Near the front of the church, a drug addict who had been saved and instantly delivered from addiction was quietly praising God—tears

134

streaming down his face. I remembered the fear I had had. Who could communicate with these addicts, with the fear-filled families locked in their apartments, buried in a jungle of concrete and steel? He could, He had, and He still was—and some of them were sitting right here praising God.

"This is my blood of the new covenant which is shed for you."

The deacons moved again among the people. Someone began to sing, and the congregation joined, as one man. The Holy Spirit seemed to breathe upon us and bend us like trees before a summer breeze. The rustle of His Presence, glorifying Jesus. Everyone broke into song in the Spirit—oblivious of those around. Yet it was all in perfect harmony and order. There was an unseen Director.

Outside, cars began to honk their horns, and fire-crackers began to explode. And we never heard them.

At the end of the service, we all came forward and filled the aisles and front of the church. We laid hands on each other and prayed for one another. Simple recognition that we were members one of another, and needed one another. We were the Body of Christ, locally expressed—and only when we were wholly one with Him and each other, could He shine forth through us.

As we parted, praying a glorious New Year in Christ upon each other, Richard Wahlberg, one of our elders, came to me praising God. He said, "You know, I feel like this is just the beginning. We are on tip-toe waiting for the starter's gun. We haven't seen anything yet."

I smiled and went into my office. I sat on the floor and said—"Amen, Brother Richard, Amen."

– NOTES –

– NOTES –

– NOTES –

– NOTES –

– NOTES –

– NOTES –

– NOTES –

– NOTES –

– NOTES –

– NOTES –

**Now you can hear famous authors...recorded live...
telling of a personal experience or testimony**

$3.95   # CASSETTES $3.95

COMPLETE NEW TESTAMENT KING JAMES VERSION
15 CASSETTES $59.95

JB1	JAMES BJORNSTADT, Author of "20th CENTURY PROPHECY"
SBC	RENEWAL IN SONG—Sampler Psalms
TA1	NICKY CRUZ, Author of "RUN BABY RUN"
TA2	(LTC) MERLIN CAROTHERS, Author of "PRISON TO PRAISE"
TA3	JAMIE BUCKINGHAM, co-author of "RUN BABY RUN"
TA4	ARTHUR KATZ, Author of "BEN ISRAEL"
TA5	DENNIS BENNETT, Author of "NINE O'CLOCK IN THE MORNING"
TA6	BOB BARTLETT, Author of "THE SOUL PATROL"
TA7	DR. RAY JARMAN, Author of "THE GRACE AND THE GLORY OF GOD"
TA8	MICHAEL HARPER, Author of "WALK IN THE SPIRIT"
TA9	BOB MUMFORD, Author of "15 STEPS OUT"
TA10	DR. HOBART FREEMAN, Author of "ANGELS OF LIGHT?"
TA11	DAVID duPLESSIS, Author of "THE SPIRIT BADE ME GO"
TA12	WENDELL WALLACE, Author of "BORN TO BURN"
TA13	DR. HOWARD ERVIN, Author of "THESE ARE NOT DRUNKEN"
TA14	CLINTON WHITE, Author of "FROM THE BELLY OF THE WHALE"
TA15	DR. ROBERT FROST, Author of "AGLOW WITH THE SPIRIT"
TA16	DR. J. RODMAN WILLIAMS, Author of "THE ERA OF THE SPIRIT"

TA17 SONNY ARGUINZONI, Author of "GOD'S JUNKIE"

TA18 KATHRYN KUHLMAN — "AN HOUR WITH KATHRYN KUHLMAN"

TA19 KEVIN RANAGHAN, Author of "CATHOLIC PENTE—COSTALS"

TA20 CHARLES SIMPSON — "A SOUTHERN BAPTIST LOOKS AT PENTECOST"

TA21 WILLARD CANTELON — "THE NEW WORLD MONEY SYSTEM"

TA22 THE CHARISMATIC RENEWAL—Bredesen, Ervin, Evans, Brown, Roberts

TA23 FR. JOSEPH ORSINI, Author of "HEAR MY CONFESSION"

TA24 PHIL SAINT, Author of "AMAZING SAINTS"

TA25 PAT ROBERTSON, Author of "SHOUT IT FROM THE HOUSETOPS"

TA26 MALCOLM SMITH, Author of "TURN YOUR BACK ON THE PROBLEM"

TA27 FRANK FOGLIO, Author of "HEY, GOD!"

RECORDS — $4.95

MS120 AN HOUR WITH KATHRYN KUHLMAN

M7 NICKY CRUZ — 7" record

M13-72 NICKY CRUZ — 12" record

M125 NEW WORLD MONEY SYSTEM — Willard Cantelon

order from your local bookstore
or W.B.S.
Box 292
Watchung, N.J. 07061

Title	Code	Price
A NEW SONG—Boone	AA3	$ .95
AGLOW WITH THE SPIRIT—Frost	L326	.95
AMAZING SAINTS—Saint	L409	2.50
AND FORBID NOT TO SPEAK—Ervin	L329	.95
AND SIGNS FOLLOWED—Price	P002	1.50
ANGLES OF LIGHT?—Freeman	A506	.95
ANSWERS TO PRAISE—Carothers	L670	1.95
ARMSTRONG ERROR—DeLoach	L317	.95
AS AT THE BEGINNING—Harper	L721	1.95
BAPTISM IN THE SPIRIT—Schep	L343	1.50
BAPTISM IN THE SPIRIT—BIBLICAL —Cockburn	16F	.65
BAPTISM OF FIRE—Harper	8F	.60
BAPTIZED IN ONE SPIRIT—Baker	1F	.60
BAPTIZED IN THE SPIRIT—Clark	P9	.75
BEN ISRAEL—Katz	A309	.75
BLACK TRACKS—Miles	A298	.95
BORN TO BURN—Wallace	A508	.95
CATHOLIC PENTECOSTALISM—McDonnell	P6	.60
CHALLENGING COUNTERFEIT—Gasson	L102	.95
COMING ALIVE—Buckingham	A501	.95
CONFESSIONS OF A HERETIC—Hunt	L31X	2.50
COUNSELOR TO COUNSELOR—Campbell	L335	1.50
CRISIS AMERICA—Otis	AA1	.95
DAYSPRING—White	L334	1.95
DISCOVERY (Booklet)—Frost	F71	.50
ERA OF THE SPIRIT—Williams	L322	1.95
15 STEPS OUT—Mumford	L106	1.50
FROM THE BELLY OF THE WHALE—White	A318	.95
GATHERED FOR POWER—Pulkinghm	AA4	2.50
GOD BREAKS IN—Congdon	L313	1.95

GOD IS FOR THE EMOTIONALLY ILL —Guldseth	A507	.95
GOD'S GUERRILLAS—Wilson	A152	.95
GOD'S JUNKIE—Arguinzoni	A509	.95
GOD'S LIVING ROOM—Walker	A123	.95
GONE IS SHADOWS' CHILD—Foy	L337	.95
GRACE AND THE GLORY OF GOD —Benson/Jarman	L104	1.50
HEALING ADVENTURE—White	L345	1.95
HEALING LIGHT—Sanford	L726	.95
HEAR MY CONFESSION—Orsini	L341	1.00
HEY GOD!—Goglio	P007	1.95
HOLY SPIRIT AND YOU—Bennett	L324	2.50
JESUS AND ISRAEL—Benson	A514	.95
JESUS PEOPLE ARE COMING—King	L340	1.95
JESUS PEOPLE—Pederson	AA2	.95
LAYMAN'S GUIDE TO HOLY SPIRIT—Rea	L387	2.50
LET THIS CHURCH DIE—Weaver	A520	.95
LIFE IN THE HOLY SPIRIT—Harper	5F	.50
LONELY NOW	A510	.95
LORD OF THE VALLEYS—Bulle	L018	2.50
LOST SHEPHERD—Sanford	L328	.95
MADE ALIVE—Price	P001	1.50
MANIFEST VICTORY—Moseley	L724	2.50
MIRACLES THROUGH PRAYER—Harrell	A518	.95
NICKY CRUZ GIVES THE FACTS ON DRUGS —Cruz	B70	.50
NINE O'CLOCK IN THE MORNING—Bennett	P555	2.50
NONE CAN GUESS—Harper	L722	1.95
OUT OF THIS WORLD—Fisher	A517	.95
OVERFLOWING LIFE—Frost	L327	1.75
PATHWAYS TO POWER—Davidson	L00X	1.50
PENTECOST IN THE CATHOLIC CHURCH —O'Connor	P8	.60
PENTECOSTALS—Nichol	LH711	2.50

PIONEERS OF REVIVAL—Clarke	L723	.95
POWER IN PRAISE—Carothers	L342	1.95
POWER FOR THE BODY—Harper	4F	.85
PRAYER MEETINGS—Cavnar	P2	.50
PREACHER WITH A BILLY CLUB—Asmuth	A209	.95
PRISON TO PRAISE—Carothers	A504	.95
PROPHECY A GIFT FOR THE BODY	2F	.65
PSEUDO CHRISTIANS—Jarman	A516	.95
REAL FAITH—Price	P000	1.50
RUN BABY RUN—Cruz	L101	.95
RUN BABY RUN—Cruz (Comic Book)		.20
SATAN SELLERS—Warnke	L794	2.50
SOUL PATROL—Bartlett	A500	.95
SPEAKING WITH GOD—Cantelon	L336	.95
SPIRIT BADE ME GO—DuPlessis	L325	.95
SPIRITUAL AND PHYSICAL HEALING —Price	P003	1.95
SPIRITUAL GIFTS—Clark	P3	.50
SPIRITUAL WARFARE—Harper	A505	.95
STRONGER THAN PRISON WALLS —Wurmbrand	A956	.95
TAKE ANOTHER LOOK—Mumford	L338	2.50
THERE'S MORE—Hall	L344	1.50
THESE ARE NOT DRUNKEN—Ervin	L105	2.50
THIS EARTH'S END—Benson	A513	.95
THIS WHICH YE SEE AND HEAR—Ervin	L728	1.95
TONGUES UNDER FIRE—Lillie	3F	.85
TURN YOUR BACK ON THE PROBLEM —Smith	L034	1.95
TWO WORLDS—Price	P004	1.95
UNDERGROUND SAINTS—Wurmbrand	U-1	.95
WALK IN THE SPIRIT—Harper	L319	.95
WE'VE BEEN ROBBED—Meloon	L339	1.50
YOU CAN KNOW GOD—Price	P005	.75
YOUR NEW LOOK—Buckingham	A503	.95

THE LOGOS INTERNATIONAL STUDY BIBLE

OLD AND NEW TESTAMENT: AMERICAN STANDARD VERSION
The world's finest Topical Analysis prepared by renowned scholars

WITH:--AMERICAN STANDARD TEXT (The Rock of Biblical
Integrity)
THE OLD AND NEW TESTAMENT
VARIORUM RENDERINGS*-- 150 scholars offer special
helps, suggested word trans-
lations, meanings.
TOPICAL ANALYSIS—A complete Bible analysis in one
volume.
CROSS-REFERENCES—100,000 cross-references.
INDEX, CONCORDANCE
MAPS

IN ADDITION:—THE LOGOS LAYMAN'S COMMENTARY
ON THE HOLY SPIRIT
With special reference index on every verse in the
New Testament referring to the Holy Spirit.

COMMENTARY EDITOR: **JOHN REA, Th.D.**—Biblical Research
Editor

CONTRIBUTING EDITORS: **HOWARD ERVIN, Th.D.**
RAY CORVIN, D.R.E., Ph.D.
ERWIN PRANGE, B.D.,Th.M.
DAVID du PLESSIS, D.D.
J. RODMAN WILLIAMS, Ph.D.
Fr. JOSEPH ORSINI, Ed.D.

FREE CATALOG
at religious bookstores
or
LOGOS BIBLE
185 North Avenue
Plainfield, NJ 07060

Realizing the need for a quality but easily 'understandable HOLY
SPIRIT COMMENTARY, the editors combined their efforts in
supplying a verse-by-verse analysis of the New Testament.

*Variorum renderings are alternate suggested words and phrases taken from
ancient manuscripts and offered as alternatives by leading Bible scholars.
Ancient Bible texts, their meanings, origin, and scholars' opinions are included.

Church in the Home

FREE
SAMPLE COPY
OF

LOGOS

An International Charismatic Journal

Worldwide Coverage
Feature Articles
Book Reviews
Trends

--------**WHEREVER PAPERBACKS ARE SOLD OR USE THIS COUPON**--------

WBS
Box 292, Plainfield, NJ 07061

SEND INSPIRATIONAL BOOKS LISTED BELOW

Title	Cat. No.	Price
_____	_____	_____
_____	_____	_____
_____	_____	_____
_____	_____	_____
_____	_____	_____
_____	_____	_____

☐ Send
Complete
Catalog

☐ 50c Sample
copy of the
LOGOS Journal

☐ 1 year subscription LOGOS Journal $3.00. Make payment to
WBS, Box 292, Plainfield, NJ 07061

Name _____

Street _____

City _____ State _____ Zip _____